Science & Religion

Philosophy of Religion Study Guide

Tristan Stone

First published 2014

by PushMe Press

Mid Somerset House, Southover, Wells, Somerset BA5 1UH

www.pushmepress.com

© 2014 Inducit Learning Ltd

British Library Cataloguing in Publication Data
A catalogue record for this book is available from the British Library

ISBN: 978-1-909618-42-8 (pbk)
ISBN: 978-1-910252-94-9 (hbk)
ISBN: 978-1-909618-43-5 (ebk)
ISBN: 978-1-910252-95-6 (pdf)

Typeset in Frutiger by booksellerate.com
Printed by Lightning Source

A rich and engaging community assisted by the best teachers in Philosophy

philosophy.pushmepress.com

Students and teachers explore Philosophy of Religion through handouts, film clips, presentations, case studies, extracts, games and academic articles.

Pitched just right, and so much more than a textbook, here is a place to engage with critical reflection whatever your level. Marked student essays are also posted.

Contents

Introduction - Science OR Religion?

NOMA, WHY? AND WHO?

Whenever the term "science and religion" is bandied about, many seem to immediately draw up the battle lines. Whichever camp they belong to, the presupposition is that Science and Religion are diametrically opposed and, thus, they replace "and" with "or".

This view is espoused by Stephen Jay Gould in his coining of the phrase **NOMA**, or Non-Overlapping MAgesteria.

The net, or magisterium, of science covers the EMPIRICAL realm: what is the universe made of (fact) and why does it work this way (theory). The magisterium of religion extends over questions of ultimate meaning and moral value. These two magisteria do not overlap, nor do they encompass all inquiry (consider, for example, the magisterium of art and the meaning of beauty). To cite the old clichés, science gets the age of rocks, and religion the rock of ages; science studies how the heavens go, religion how to go to heaven.

In layman's terms, this is very often posited in the assertion that "Science asks **HOW**? Religion asks **WHY**?" **RICHARD DAWKINS** (a name which, if not already familiar to you shall become so) calls this view a "tedious cliché" in his infamous 2006 book The God Delusion, correctly questioning what a "why" question is. Like much of his book, he opts for the comical **REDUCTO AD ABSURDIUM** position to make his point ("Not every English sentence beginning with the word 'why' is a legitimate question. Why are unicorns hollow?") yet it remains true that many "why?" questions can be reformulated as "what?" or "how?" questions:

> *Why did Reverend Dr Martin Luther King Jnr [MLK] give his "I have a dream" speech?*

Could be rephrased as:

> *What was MLK's plan in delivering his "I have a dream" speech?*

or

> *What were the historic, socio-economic and political causes that gave rise to the Civil Rights Movement of the mid-20th C, culminating in MLK's "I have a dream" speech?*

Which inevitably gives rise to the question:

> *Why did Americans and British white people enslave blacks?*

Or, rephrased:

> *What did Americans and British white people hope to gain by enslaving blacks? On what grounds did they hold the erroneous*

claim to racial superiority? How is it that the seemingly obvious implication of a Christian society is the axiom that God created humans in equality was ignored? What advantages did the whites have over the blacks that facilitated the barbarism of slavery?

... And so forth.

To ask "Why?" is to ask several interesting questions all at once (or one after the other). One of the questions on the Second Year Greek exam for Theology and Religious Studies at Cambridge University in 2005 was "Why did Mark's Jesus die?"

One might retort with a flippant "Because He was nailed to a cross and this led to suffocation", (a "biological" answer to the question interpreted as "What were the biological causes of Jesus' death in Mark's Gospel?"); alternatively, "Because of Roman injustice!" (to interpret the question as "What were the political machinations that led to the death of Jesus in Mark's Gospel?); or "To herald in the kingdom of God" (to interpret the question as "How does Mark present the soteriological significance and ultimate theological purpose of Jesus' death?").

One final example, cited here to highlight the misnomer that Science asks "how?" while Religion asks "Why?":

Why are we here?

Which is to say:

How have we arrived at this point?

3

or

What is the purpose of human existence?

Clearly, Science has several answers to both versions of these questions, some of which might be put as simply as:

We have arrived at this point through the process of natural and sexual selection, which we call EVOLUTION, whereby species adapt and better themselves to the point we have currently reached, vis a vis, modern man.

The purpose of human existence is to perpetuate the species and continue to evolve - physically and mentally. This may include our own scientific endeavours as we attempt to solve the EPISTEMOLOGICAL TRAUMAS of our AGNOSTICISM (which is to say, our "unknowingness").

Some religious believers may agree with these answers, to varying extents. (**CREATIONISTS** will probably not concur with the general thesis of evolution, of course.) Indeed, on the second point, **THOMAS AQUINAS**'s version of **NATURAL LAW** theology would affirm that human purpose includes a "natural inclination" to the worship of God.

WHY? is simply an umbrella term to ask the deep, searching questions that burn within us. Imagine the following conversation:

CHILD: Daddy, do I have to go to school?

FATHER: Yes.

CHILD: Why, Daddy, why?

FATHER: Because I said so.

CHILD: Why?

FATHER: Because the Law says so.

CHILD: Why?

FATHER: Because you need to be educated.

CHILD: Why?

FATHER: To answer all your "why" questions and, also, so you can get good qualifications.

CHILD: Why?

FATHER: To increase your likelihood of getting a job.

CHILD: Why?

FATHER: Because food and clothes and shelter don't come free!

CHILD: Why?

FATHER: Because we live in a capitalist society.

CHILD: Why?

FATHER: Perhaps it's because we won the last two world wars. Or perhaps it's because everyone's greedy. Or perhaps there are historic factors that I don't understand.

CHILD: Why?

FATHER: Because I don't know everything.

CHILD: Why?

FATHER: Because I'm finite.

CHILD: Why?

FATHER: I'm human. All humans are finite.

CHILD: Why?

FATHER: Perhaps we've evolved that way. Or perhaps we were created that way.

CHILD: Why?

FATHER: You're going to be late for school now. Put on your coat.

CHILD: Why?

FATHER: Because if you don't, I won't take you to the sweet shop on the way home.

... etc.

The child who asks, "why, Daddy, why?" has struck upon an interesting aspect of human inquiry - our obsession with antecedence and cause. This possibly arises from our experiences as finite beings who come to know the universe through a linear, temporal existence. Yet, because we cannot know the antecedent causes of all things, the Religious Believer posits a further question (which is also, partly, an answer to all other questions): **WHO?**

With God as the "Who" behind the "How?" "What?" "When?" and "Why?" Religion can proceed in a different direction to Science. Anti-theists will see this as a "god of the gaps" or a "Wizard of Oz", whereas the theist sees this as a reasonable hypothesis which answers some questions and asks further, yet more interesting ones. This does not mean that religious believers ditch the "old" questions, but they may say that the "Who?" questions supersede and complement them. It is from this position that we can truly start to talk about Science AND Religion.

A FALSE DICHOTOMY - HORSES FOR COURSES

Those who posit the NOMA thesis do so on the assumption of a false dichotomy between science and religion. It is far more likely that there are certain questions which the theologian asks that the scientist has little or no interest in (where scientist is taken to mean empiricist or materialist). This is simply a case of horses for courses. In the same way that you would not go to your doctor to ask him whether you should stick with the same car insurer, so you would not ask a scientist whether we are saved by faith in Christ or the faithfulness of Christ. By the same token, few theologians are qualified to explain Einstein's theory of special relativity. Of course there are scientists who are theologians and theologians who are scientists.

Both fields are attempting to solve our **EPISTEMOLOGICAL TRAUMA** (arising from the fact that we cannot, or do not, know).

However, even though Dawkins might not be a proponent of NOMA, his claim that "I have yet to see any good reason to suppose that theology (as opposed to biblical history, literature, etc) is a subject at all" is certainly the proverbial blue touch paper to many believers - and probably intentionally so.

One of Dawkins' main theses in The God Delusion is that "the presence or absence of a creative super-intelligence is unequivocally a scientific question, even if it is not in practice - or not yet - a decided one." As such, he goes on to argue that the "God hypothesis" can be shown to be almost certainly false. This begs the question, "What is meant by a 'scientific' question?"

EMPIRICISM

A common misconception of Science is that it is **OBJECTIVE**. This has helped to perpetuate the false dichotomy between religion and science - because religion claims belief in the supernatural, all know theological claims to be biased. However, the opposite is surely true: that Dawkins is an ardent self-confessed atheist who says of his God Delusion "If this book works as I intend, religious readers who open it will be atheists when they put it down" should sound alarm bells - this is not a disinterested party; this is someone with an agenda. Dawkins seeks to proselytise as much as the Christian missionary. His assertion that "dyed-in-the-wool faith-heads are immune to argument" serves to brand anyone who may disagree with him an irrational, "unscientific", blind idiot. Such polemic is surely to be avoided from a disinterested, scientific perspective. At best, it fails to accept that some religious believers' faith has recourse to "science" or, rather, empiricism.

What is empiricism?

EMPIRICISM, in philosophy, is the view that all concepts originate in experience, that all concepts are about or applicable to things that can be experienced, or that all rationally acceptable beliefs or propositions are justifiable or knowable only through experience. This broad definition accords with the derivation of the term empiricism from the ancient Greek word empeiria, meaning "experience".

Put simply, empiricism is one aspect of knowledge - based on what we can perceive with our senses and/or measure. Scientific methodology is based on empiricism: experiments are conducted to test a hypothesis. By observing and measuring results, conclusions are drawn.

To test the temperature at which water boils, a heat source and a thermometer are applied to a water container. The experimenter would record the temperature reached at the point the water started to boil and conclude it was in the region of 100 degrees Celsius.

EPISTEMOLOGY - OR "HOW WE KNOW WHAT WE KNOW"

Epistemology is concerned with how we know things. Of course, the old proverb that the difference between the fool and the wise man is that "the fool knows not, and knows not that he knows not; the wise knows not, and knows that he knows not" was not lost on the greatest philosophers: **SOCRATES'** famous claim that "all I know is that I know nothing" is the basis for the Socratic Method. If the epistemological trauma of the human condition is that we do not (and, perhaps cannot) know, then to what extent can empiricism be our saviour?

The introduction to Alfred Lord Tennyson's elegy "In Memoriam" has this pithy reiteration of the problem:

> Our little systems have their day;
> They have their day and cease to be;
> They are but broken lights of Thee,
> And Thou, O Lord, art more than they.
>
> We have but faith: we cannot know;
> For knowledge is of things we see;
> And yet we trust it comes from Thee,
> A beam in darkness: let it grow.

Or, as St Paul has it in that famous passage from his first letter to the church in Corinth (Corinthians 13:8-9, 12):

> Where there is knowledge, it will pass away. For we know in part and we prophesy in part ... now we see the the mirror,

dimly then we shall see face to face. Now I know in part; then I shall know fully, even as I am fully known.

Of course, the "then" refers to the **ESCHATON** - the life to come in Shakespeare's "Undiscovered Country" after the "mortal coil" has been "shuffled off" (ie after death).

Essentially, the Religious and Scientific approaches are both agnostically hopeful: both positions recognise that our knowledge is, at present, limited, and both believe that the epistemological trauma will be resolved - either with recourse to empiricism, or revelation. Dawkins and his ilk would hope that Science will eventually unravel every mystery of the universe; St Paul holds that we shall find out after death.

Both of these positions claim recourse to the **IMAGINAL** - which is to say, to something as yet unknowable but that can be imagined, or conceived of.

This highlights two important points:

- **ESCHATOLOGICAL VERIFICATION** is common to Science and Religion.

- Philosophy of Religion is a synthesis.

How do we know that the water is hot? How do you know that your friends care about you or that a triangle has three sides? The **LOGICAL POSITIVISTS** held that statements are only meaningful if they can be verified **SYNTHETICALLY** or **ANALYTICALLY**. The most famous group of logical positivists was a collective self-designated as the **VIENNA CIRCLE** in the early 20th C. Members included **LUDWIG WITTGENSTEIN, MORITZ SCHLICK** and **RUDOLF CARNAP**.

A statement is synthetic if it can be verified **A POSTERIORI** (after experience). An analytic statement is verified **A PRIORI** (before or without experience):

"The water is hot" is meaningful because you can put your hand on it and sense the temperature, or measure it with a thermometer. It is a synthetic statement.

"A triangle has three sides" is meaningful because it is true by definition - a triangle is a shape with (only) three sides. It is an analytic statement.

"My friends care about me" is not meaningful because it is not analytically or synthetically verifiable - just because they might do "nice" or "kind" things does not empirically verify their feelings.

AJ AYER and the Vienna Circle concluded that all metaphorical and religious language was meaningless.

Incidentally, it is worth noting that most analytically true statements are **TAUTOLOGIES** - simply ways of repeating the same information: eg, a bachelor is an unmarried man (by definition).

Examples of common tautologies today are:

- PIN number (Personal Identification Number Number)

- ATM machine (Auto Teller Machine Machine)

However, as **JOHN HICK** points out, many religious statements are verifiable in principle eschatologically (after death/at the end of the world). According to his eschatological verification principle, the question of God's existence could be verified after death. If we die and go to heaven, the question will be answered in the affirmative.

If, on the other hand, there is neither God nor afterlife, we shan't know, because we will simply cease to exist. This is most commonly over-simplified as **PASCHAL'S WAGER**.

By the same token, although we might not currently know whether there is intelligent life elsewhere in the universe (a "scientific" question), it is hoped that there will be an answer some day. In this respect, both the Scientist and the Theologian use eschatological verification as a matter of course; they merely disagree about the nature of the eschaton.

You might be wondering why, in a Study Guide ostensibly about Science and Religion, we seem to have digressed into Religious Language. This highlights the second point:

The Philosopher of Religion cannot simply talk about "the problem of evil" or "the existence of God" or "Science and Religion" - they are all in **SYNTHESIS**. It is a vulgar peculiarity of exam boards to divide papers on Philosophy of Religion into "units". This compartmentalisation of Philosophy into topics belies the synthetic nature of the subject. This book will seek to draw attention to the areas that cross over while retaining a focus on Science and Religion.

There is a further point: although it is very difficult to talk of "the problem of suffering" without reference to "free will" and a concept of God, therefore as Creator, it is possible to be a marine biologist and not write a sentence on the Hadron Collider. I should not be surprised if a theoretical physicist had not dissected a frog since GCSE Science. That is because, although the methodology of science (empiricism) is common to all its branches (indeed, arguably what makes it "science" at all), biology, chemistry and physics are asking sometimes similar, sometimes vastly different questions. Perhaps this brings us back to the WHY.

Science does not need Philosophy or Theology to work out the mass of hydrogen, but Philosophy needs to engage with science and all other human disciplines if it is to answer its questions because its questions are, perhaps, less specific.

KARL BARTH (1886-1968), one of the most prolific and pre-eminent Protestant theologians of the 20th C, pithily struck this nail on its head when he wrote in the second edition of Romans:

> *All human achievements are little more than Prolegomena [prologues/introductions] and this is especially the case in the field of theology.*

THE PRESUMPTION OF EMPIRICISM

> *What is real? How do you define real? If you're talking about what you can feel, what you can smell, what you can taste and see, then real is simply electrical signals interpreted by your brain.* - Morpheus in The Matrix (Wachowski Brothers, 1999)

If the first axiom of Religious Faith is "I believe in what I cannot see", then Scientific Inquiry's first axiom might be "I believe in what I can see."

Whatever system we adopt for resolving our epistemological trauma, we must have a starting point, and empiricism's is certainly the assumption that we can trust our senses (where we do not believe our senses to have been deceived) and that reality can be accessed through the material world.

This is, in philosophical terms, a **REALIST** approach to truth. Dawkins is almost certainly a realist. Most people are, in fact, realists.

The **REALIST** position holds that there is, "out there", an objective truth. Either there IS or IS NOT a God. Dawkins would argue that there probably is not a God.

The **ANTI-REALIST** is a post-modern animal who subjectifies truth. To the anti-realist, there neither is, nor is not a God. Only that, to theists, God exists and to atheists, He does not. By this view, it is true within Islam to say "Muhammad is the Messenger of Allah" and within Christianity to say "Jesus is the incarnate Second Person of the Trinity".

This might remind you of Wittgenstein's language games and, again, we find that the "science and religion topic" also needs to make recourse to a study of religious language.

This anti-realist view of the world, and indeed truth, is concisely explained by Tom Stoppard, through the character of the Player King in Act II of his famous play Rosencrantz and Guildernstern Are Dead:

> *Player: For all anyone knows nothing is [true]. Everything has to be taken on trust: truth is only that which is taken to be true. It's the currency of living. There may be nothing behind it, but it doesn't make any difference so long as it is honoured. One acts on assumptions. What do you assume?*

To return to The Matrix, it is not beyond the scope of reason to posit that we are all living in a simulacrum, created by some super-human (though not necessarily supernatural) intelligence. Dawkins himself recognises that this cannot be falsified. Whether or not it is true, from the realist perspective, however may not matter - we might not be able to do anything about our plight.

THE (UN)FALSIFIABILITY PRINCIPLE /DEMARCATION

We learn from our mistakes; and this means that when we arrive at inconsistencies we turn back, and reframe our assumptions. - Karl Popper, The Open Universe, p.108

The question of unfalsifiability is of paramount significance. **KARL POPPER** (1902-1994) advanced the idea that, although scientific theories cannot be proven, they can be falsified.

For example, imagine trying to prove that all the apples in the world are green. This would be practically impossible! But, if you find one red apple, you can show that not all the apples in the world are green.

You have, therefore, falsified the hypothesis.

Popper argued that the **DEMARCATION** of science (ie the distinguishing feature that separates science from other forms of inquiry) is that scientific questions are falsifiable. If it is **UNFALSIFIABLE**, Popper holds that it is unscientific.

By this criterion, many religious claims would be deemed "unscientific" because they are unfalsifiable:

One of the most obvious examples comes from the Church of Jesus Christ of the Latter Day Saints (the "Mormons"). Its founder, Joseph Smith (1805-1844) claimed, following several encounters with with "two personages", to have been directed by an angel ("the resurrected being Moroni") to some buried golden plates on 21 September 1823, which he translated into English. This became known as "The Book of Mormon" and was published in 1830.

Smith made annual visits to the hill where the plates where buried, but said that he was prevented from removing them by the angel. However, on his fourth annual visit (1827), Smith returned home with a heavy object, wrapped in cloth, which he put in a box. People were permitted to see the box, but Smith insisted that the angel had forbidden anyone from seeing the actual plates until they had been translated into English (from a pseudo-Egyptian). This he achieved with recourse to a seer stone placed in a hat over his face. (According to the introduction of The Book of Mormon, Smith translated the plates "by the gift and power of God".) Although "the Lord provided for eleven others to see the gold plates for themselves" and their two signed testimonies are found in The Book of Mormon, Smith said he returned the plates, after translation, to the angel Moroni.

Thus no record of the plates currently exists and his story cannot be falsified. It therefore fails Popper's test and is not scientific.

Many more religious stories - particularly, of course, **MIRACLES** - are similarly unfalsifiable and some more will be examined later in subsequent chapters.

One further thing worth noting is that Popper did not go so far as to say that theories that are not falsifiable are meaningless, merely that they are not scientific.

Students of religious language will be familiar with RM Hare's term **BLIK** - meaning an unfalsifiable conviction held that may be true or fallacious. This is usually applied (negatively) to religious belief but, as we have seen in recent news, scientists are often likely to distrust evidence, even within their own field, if it goes against their hypotheses. Professor Neil Turok is yet to acknowledge that recent evidence in support of Stephen Hawking's model of the Big Bang disproves Turok's belief in a series of big bangs and multiple universes.

KEY TERMS

- **A POSTERIORI** - From experience. Reasoning is a posteriori if it is based on experience.

- **A PRIORI** - Without experience. Reasoning is a priori if it makes no recourse to experience

- **AGNOSTIC** - Literally "no knowledge" or "without knowledge". Agnostics either claim to be undecided about believing in God or say we cannot know.

- **ANALYTIC** - Statements are analytic if they do not appeal to experience, eg "A triangle has three sides." (They are often tautologies.)

- **ANTI-REALIST** - The view that truth is relative. For example, it is true that Muhammad is the prophet within Islam but not Judaism.

- **BLIK** - Coined by RM Hare, this is a falsifiable conviction held by someone. Note - it is not necessarily untrue.

- **EMPIRICAL (EMPIRICISM)** - Empirical evidence comprises of data drawn from sensory experience. Empiricism is concerned with what is externally observable or measurable and thus verifiable.

- **EPISTEMOLOGY (EPISTEMOLOGICAL TRAUMA)** - The study of knowledge. The "epistemological trauma of the human condition" referred to in this book is the limit of human knowledge - ie that we cannot know.

- **ESCHATOLOGICAL VERIFICATION (ESCHATON)** - Eschaton means "end" or "beyond". It is the point after death or the end of the world. Eschatological verification is the idea that, although something might not be verified now, it will be in the future. This makes it meaningful to say "the Queen will visit Broadstairs on Thursday" because we can verify this on Thursday, if not now.

- **EVOLUTION** - The widely held view that living beings gradually adapt to their environment over time and favourable genetic mutations that aid survival add to improvements in DNA.

- **FALSIFIABLE** - A claim is falsifiable if it is known what evidence would count against it. For example "all swans are white" is falsified by the discovery of a black swan.

- **IMAGINAL** - With recourse to the imagination but not made up - employing that part of the mind that looks beyond what is presently seen/known/available.

- **LOGICAL POSITIVISM** - Closely linked to verification, the logical positivists tried to rid us of "meaningless language".

- **MAGESTERIUM (PLURAL - MAGESTERIA)** - "Net" or domain of teaching authority.

- **NOMA** - Non Overlapping Magesteria - the view that Science and Religion are completely separate entities.

- **REALIST** - The view that there is objective truth and reality, eg either there is OR is not a God.

- **REDUCTO AD ABSURDIUM** - Reducing an argument to absurdity.

- **SYNTHETIC** - A statement is synthetic if it requires experience to make it, eg "John is a bachelor." We must have knowledge of John to know if this is true or false.

- **UNFALSIFIABLE** - A statement is unfalsifiable if nothing can be conceived of which would count against it.

SELF-ASSESSMENT QUESTIONS

1. What is Science?

2. What is Religion?

3. Explain why Dawkins regards it a "tedious cliché" to say that "science asks how, religion asks why".

4. How important do you think religious language and other areas of the Philosophy of Religion are to the topic of Science and Religion?

5. Does empiricism have its limits?

6. Do you consider yourself a realist or an anti-realist?

7. How far would you agree with Dawkins's assertion that "the God hypothesis" is a "scientific question"?

8. Explain how Popper's falsification principle demarcates science from other disciplines.

9. Write an article of 1,000 words explaining to what extent eschatological verification is common to the Scientific and Religious projects.

10. "Bliks show that there is no real difference between faith in the supernatural and faith in the natural." To what extent do you agree?

Origins

THE BIG BANG THEORY

The Big Bang theory is the most widely accepted scientific explanation for the origins of the universe. It holds that all matter currently existing originated from a single event, approximately 13.798 ± 0.037 billion years ago. It is derived from observations of space and, as such, is a relatively new concept (owing to the great strides in telescopic advances, physics and so forth).

In the early 20th C, **ALBERT EINSTEIN** (1879-1955) had proposed that the universe was **STATIC** - ie infinite spatially and temporally, neither expanding nor contracting. However, **GEORGES LEMAÎTRE** (1894-1966), a Roman Catholic Monseigneur and professor of physics, suggested, in 1925, that the universe was, in fact, expanding, based on work relating to **RED SHIFT**.

Red shift

The **DOPPLER EFFECT** holds that when a source of light or sound waves moves towards an observer, the observed wavelength is decreased and the frequency increased. The opposite occurs when the source of the waves moves further from the observer - the observed wavelength is increased and the frequency decreased. This is the reason why cars and, particularly, sirens, appear to "bend" in pitch as they come towards us and depart.

In 1929, **EDWIN HUBBLE** formulated his version of the Red Shift Distance Law (now known as "Hubble's Law", despite Lemaître's prior claim to the discovery) which states that "the red shifts in the spectra of distant galaxies (and hence their speeds of recession) are proportional to their distance". Moreover, as we observe the galaxies and star clusters farthest from us, they appear to have a higher velocity. Thus, all parts of the universe that can be observed are receding from each other. This means that there was a point from which they began to recede.

The "Big Bang" holds, then, that the universe started from a single point of origin, when subatomic particles collided, causing a chain reaction. This is known as t=0 and is, essentially, the starting point of space and time. The explosion generated heat and, as it cooled, matter formed and stars and galaxies were born, eventually culminating (for our purposes) in the formation of our solar system and the planet Earth.

What caused the Big Bang?

In short, this remains unknown. Some contemporary physicists suggest that our universe is one of several, contained in a "multiverse". Many religious believers welcome the Big Bang theory as evidence supporting the notion of a finite universe with a clear beginning. As no one is able to explain where the particles came from that caused the Big Bang, God seems a likely candidate to many.

Certainly, the Big Bang theory and Creation are not incompatible - the former could simply be the methodology used by the Creator. For example, if I were to tell you that I baked a cake yesterday, I do not need to go into the minutiae of how I sieved the flour, selected the recipe or purchased the eggs. The accounts of Creation in Scripture are not intended to be science manuals - they establish the dependence of the created upon the Creator.

Proponents of cosmological arguments for the existence of God might also use the Big Bang theory in refuting a notion of **INFINITE REGRESS**, thereby demonstrating the necessity of a **FIRST CAUSE** of the universe that is not, itself, the universe:

P1 All finite things have a cause.

P2 The Big Bang theory demonstrates that the universe is finite.

P3 The universe cannot cause itself.

P4 Whatever caused the universe cannot be finite or the universe.

C There is a FIRST CAUSE to the universe that we call God.

For some, the leap from First Cause to Creator is too great, and while it is certain that not all proponents of the Big Bang theory believe God is "behind it", and that not all theists believe the Big Bang to be the method employed by the Creator, the two explanations are by no means incompatible and, in the absence of a narrative from science as to what caused the Big Bang, many chalk it up to a Creator.

CREATION

In the beginning God created the heavens and the earth. 2 Now the earth was formless and empty, darkness was over the surface of the deep, and the Spirit of God was hovering over the waters.

3 And God said, "Let there be light," and there was light. 4 God saw that the light was good, and he separated the light from the darkness. 5 God called the light "day", and the darkness he called "night". And there was evening, and there was morning - the first day. - Genesis 1:1-5, NIV

Much ink has been poured over the familiar opening to Genesis - the first book of the Torah and the Bible respectively. Many people read it as a literal account of the origins of the world (and, by extension, the universe); others give it a metaphorical or symbolic reading. Inevitably, many scientists have set about trying to verify or falsify its literal, historical veracity.

Literal interpretations

Literal interpretations of Genesis are difficult for two reasons:

1. There seems to be an incongruity with current empirical, geological and biological evidence about the age of the earth and the process of evolution (ie science "disproves" Genesis, or perhaps falsifies it - yet if science falsifies it, does it make Genesis a scientific claim that it is erroneous?).

2. There seems to be an internal incongruity within the first two chapters (ie there are two "different" accounts of creation found in Genesis 1 and 2).

Examining each in turn:

▸ **The basic order for the creation of the universe in Genesis 1 is as follows**

Day	Creative Act
"In the beginning"	*God creates heavens and earth*
1	*God separates light from dark*
2	*God separates sky from sea*
3	*God separates land from sea* *God commands the earth to produce vegetation* *and trees*
4	*God makes the sun, moon and stars*
5	*God creates sea life, then birds*
6	*God creates animals (mammals and other creatures* *on the earth) and, lastly, humans, "in the image* *of God"* *God gives human beings authority over the earth* *and its creatures. Tells them to multiply*
7	*God rests from His creative work*

Aside from the claim that a supernatural agent is behind the origins of the universe, earth and life (of course, the quintessential tenet of faith and main point of Genesis for the religious believer), the details of the account present some scientific problems:

- The "age" of the universe would seem to be significantly "younger" than the (approximately) 13.72 billion years currently espoused by the scientific community.

- "Day 4" is particularly problematic, as this would seem to suggest that the earth existed independently of the sun and the moon.

- Humans are believed to be a distinctly separate creation, which goes against evolutionary theories.

In response, religious believers might argue that the word "day" in English translations is not an accurate rendering of the Hebrew word "yom". Linguistically, several scholars argue that the word has several meanings, including:

- 24 hours

- an indefinite period of time, or an "age"

- a period of light (as opposed to darkness)

- a particular "moment" in time

- a year.

Arguments from scripture often refer to Psalm 90, verse 4:

> A thousand years in your sight are like a day that has just gone by, or like a watch in the night.

If God is infinite and no humans were created until the end of the "sixth day", then the usage of the word "yom" is referring to time from "God's perspective". **ST AUGUSTINE OF HIPPO** (354-430) has a pithy passage about time from God's perspective in Book XI of his Confessions:

> *Your years are completely present to you all at once, because they are at a permanent standstill. They do not move on, forced to give way before the advance of others, because they never pass at all. But our years will all be complete only when they have all moved into the past. Your years are one day, yet your day does not come daily but is always today, because your today does not give place to any tomorrow nor does it take the place of any yesterday. Your today is eternity.*

Either, or both of these arguments mean that believers can still maintain the authority of the Genesis account, while accepting current scientific evidence. Some believers might still maintain this should be read "literally" and simply point out that the literal meaning of "yom" in this context is not 24 hours.

Of course, there are still many exponents of the "Young Earth" theory and these are generally (though not always) found in parts of America and often belong to the "Creationist lobby" so often derided and reviled by Dawkins et al.

Historically, this has given rise to the geocentric model of the universe: the fallacious belief that the earth is at the centre of the universe and that the sun orbits the earth.

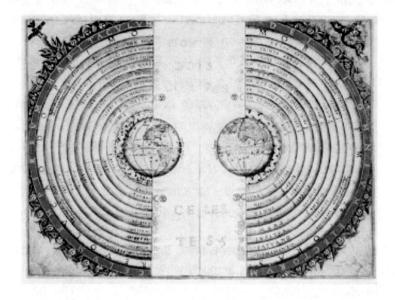

The Ptolemaic geocentric model of the universe according to the Portuguese cosmographer and cartographer Bartolomeu Velho (Bibliothèque Nationale de France, Paris)

Many anti-theists cite the trial of **GALILEO GALILEI** in the 17th C as epitomising the Church's refusal to accept empirical evidence that contradicts doctrine (Church teaching). Of course, this just demonstrates that, in the absence of good science, bad theology will prevail (where bad theology means making scientific and literal readings of translations of scripture). One could also argue it was "bad science" and that the fact that no serious theologian or scientist now accepts the geocentric fallacy demonstrates that religion is not simply unbending but leaves "the jury out" on scientific matters for a little longer if it challenges the status quo.

Nevertheless, a literal interpretation of the fourth day of creation remains a problem in light of physics: how can the earth spin on its axis and so forth without a sun to orbit? It is possible that some might still argue that it did not need to orbit the earth until creatures inhabited it although, of course, such assertions are difficult to reason philosophically, theologically or empirically.

We shall look at **EVOLUTION** later, but suffice it to say at this point that most religious believers who defend the creation of humans "in the image of God" (ie as a distinctive act apart from evolution) simply deny the veracity of evolutionary theory, either on the macro or micro level. Their arguments generally take some of the following forms:

- lack of conclusive empirical evidence for evolution

- the "gaps" in Darwinist theory

- evolution is merely another meta-narrative in the same way that Genesis is

- the theological prima facie conviction that we are spiritual creatures.

The rest of the Bible seems to presuppose the "special" nature of humanity; if we are merely "evolved" primates this might negate revelation, sin and salvation - ie it undermines the entire Judeo-Christian meta-narrative.

▶ There seems to be a discrepancy between the first two chapters of Genesis

WHEN?	GENESIS 1	CREATIVE ACTS ACCORDING TO GENESIS 1:
"In the beginning"	*1:1*	*God creates heavens and earth*
Day 1	*Gen 1:2-5*	*God separates light from dark*
Day 2	*Gen 1:6-8*	*God separates sky from sea*
Day 3	*Gen 1:9-13*	*God separates land from sea God commands the earth to produce vegetation and trees*
Day 4	*Gen 1:14-19*	*God makes the sun, moon and stars*
Day 5	*Gen 1:20-23*	*God creates sea life, then birds*
Day 6	*Gen 1:24-31*	*God creates animals (mammals and other creatures on the earth) and, lastly, humans, "in the image of God" God gives human beings authority over the earth and its creatures and tells them to multiply*
Day 7	*Gen 2:1-4*	*God rests from His creative work*

WHEN?	GENESIS 2:4B	CREATIVE ACTS ACCORDING TO GENESIS 2:
"In the day that the Lord God made the earth and heavens"		*No rain falls. Instead, water (dew) "rises" up and nourishes the earth* *God forms man from the dust and breathes "life" into his nostrils*
Afterwards ...	*Gen 2:8*	*God plants a garden (Eden) "in the East" and places the man in it*
Afterwards ...	*Gen 2:9a*	*God causes trees of every kind to come out of the ground*
Then ...	*Gen 2:9b-17*	*In the centre of the garden is placed the tree of life and the tree of the knowledge of good and evil* *God commands the man not to eat of these trees* *He is to till the land and eat everything else*
Some time later?	*Gen 2:18-20*	*God creates all the animals and birds "out of the ground" as companions for the man* *Man names all the animals*
Later still	*Gen 2:21-24*	*Seeing that man is still lonely, God causes him to fall asleep* *Taking a rib from the man, God makes woman who becomes his wife*

It seems patently obvious, upon first inspection, that the two accounts contradict each other - namely that the creation of "man" precedes that of vegetation and animals in Genesis 2, while man is the culmination of creation (a little like the pinnacle of evolution) in Genesis 1.

Many **CREATIONISTS** and supporters of literal interpretations of the Bible attempt to reconcile these differences. Some are more sophisticated than others but basically follow the same line - namely, that Genesis 2:4-24 offers a further, detailed account of the "sixth day" of Genesis 1:24-31. The following is a summary of one such attempt taken from an online article which you can read by following the link below:

> Genesis 2:4–25 "zooms in on day six and shows some of the events of that day".

> The creation of the plants and shrubs in Genesis 2 are specific to the garden and different from the general trees and plants created on the "third day" of Genesis 1.

> The translation into English of the verb "formed" has erroneously been given the perfect tense in many versions of the Bible. The original Hebrew "yatsar" is better translated in this passage in its PLUPERFECT form (ie "it had happened" - already, that is, in the past).

> Therefore, in the NIV, Genesis 2:19 is rendered: "Now the LORD God had formed out of the ground all the beasts of the field and all the birds of the air." - answersingenesis.org

Whether or not you are convinced by this argument, it highlights a very real problem for religious believers: much meaning is lost, or changed, in translation. We are back to the old chestnut of religious language. This is undoubtedly why Muslims insist that translations of the Qur'an can only ever be interpretations, and why many Muslims learn the Qur'an in its original Arabic.

Non-literal interpretations

Of course, not all religious believers claim a literal interpretation of the Genesis account(s). Indeed, there are many (arguably the majority, particularly in the UK) Jews and Christians who, rather, draw from Genesis the quintessential theological truth that God is the author of all that is.

More importantly, Genesis tells believers that God creates **EX NIHILO** (out of nothing). Thus St Augustine writes:

> Those who ask "What was God doing before he made heaven and earth?" are still steeped in error which they should have discarded.

This doctrine of creation ex nihilo is actually rather reasonable, for, as Augustine demonstrates: "Nor was it in the universe that you made the universe, because until the universe was made there was no place where it could be made." Therefore, all that is has been made "not from God's own substance, but from nothing."

Books XI-XIII of his Confessions offer interesting interpretations on the Genesis account and are worth reading, as are the Questions on the six days of creation in Aquinas's Summa Theologica. Atheists may find Aquinas's general repost "Suffices the authority of Scripture" annoying but, upon a careful reading and allowing for the lack of "scientific" knowledge in his century, most will find he is more sophisticated than someone who simply repeats English (or Latin) translations of the Bible parrot-fashion.

Indeed, Aquinas's famous, and often misunderstood, work in an earlier part of the Summa Theologica is worth mentioning. Most commonly and erroneously (cf Dawkins) referred to as Aquinas's "proofs" for the existence of God, Aquinas offers five "ways" to demonstrate the existence of God in Question 2, Article 3 of the Summa Theologica. The first three ways are extremely similar and are really different ways of looking at the same mode of demonstration - namely, by positing God as the answer to an almost mathematical equation, whereby all things that are in motion, or are caused or are contingent have been put in motion, been caused and owe their contingency to a prime mover, first cause or necessary being. These Ways are not necessarily meant to refer to a chronological dependence but, rather, a more general contingency. So, the purpose of Genesis, according to this sort of interpretation, establishes the Creation's contingency on God as its progenitor and sustainer.

The last point is an important one that **RENÉ DESCARTES** (1596-1650) makes in his third Meditation:

> It is clear to anyone who thinks about the nature of times that the same power and action is obviously required to conserve anything during the individual moments of its duration as would be required to create it for the first time, had it not already existed, thus there is only a distinction of reason between conservation and creation, and this is one of the things that are evident by the natural light of reason.

Therefore, I should now ask myself: have I some power by which I can bring it about that I, who exist at present, will still exist a short time in the future? Since I am only a thinking thing or, at least, I am discussing only those features of that part of me which is specifically a thinking thing, if I had such a power I would undoubtedly by aware of it. But I do not experience any such power, and therefore I know very evidently that I depend on some being that is distinct from me.

Thus, Genesis not merely establishes God as He would made us, but also He who conserves (or sustains) us. This banishes **DEISM**: God does not simply "roll the dice" and sit back but is still active in Creation. Indeed, some scholars observe that there is not "end" to the seventh (Sabbath) day in Genesis. Unlike the others which have "and it was evening and morning the nth day" there seems to be no conclusion to the seventh day.

The essential thing to draw from all this that human beings are **CREATURES** and owe their being to an Ultimate, Necessary Being (ie God). Genesis 1-3 sets up the entire Judeo-Christian framework about the condition of man in his state of relationship to God. The Bible is, essentially, a meta-narrative describing the evolution of that **RELATIONSHIP** - whether interpreted literally or metaphorically.

As soon as we start speaking of relationship, we are, inexorably drawn back to the previous observation that religious questions are often concerned with **WHO?**

Of course, while non-literal interpretations of the Bible seem liberal or rational in a post-Enlightenment age to a believer who has an inkling of Darwin, and while this might enable the believer to have a "foot in both camps", the questions as to the process of Creation are still, largely unanswered. If the "Fall" of Genesis 3 is only a metaphor, what is it a metaphor for? If God did not make man "in His own image", how can the non-literalist explain or describe the special relationship between God and man?

MAN

Defining man

What a piece of work is a man! How noble in reason, how infinite in faculty! In form and moving how express and admirable! In action how like an angel, in apprehension how like a god! The beauty of the world. The paragon of animals. And yet, to me, what is this quintessence of dust? - William Shakespeare, Hamlet, Act II, scene ii

Element	Percentage in body
Oxygen	65
Carbon	18
Hydrogen	10
Nitrogen	3
Others	4

The composition of the human body

There is a joke told about the materialist and God who are discussing the creation of man:

MATERIALIST: Well, you think you're so great, creating man "out of the dust". I know what you're about - human beings are simply a collection of elements.

GOD: So you think think you're as good as me?

MATERIALIST: If what makes you "God" is that you can make man out of the dust, then, yeah! I just need some carbon, hydrogen ...

GOD: Wait a minute.

MATERIALIST: What?

GOD: First, make your own dust.

Again, this highlights the importance of the religious belief of creation ex nihilo and also brings us back to **NOMA**.

When someone asks of the Scientist and the Religious Believer "What is man?" they very well might interpret the question differently. The Scientist might take it to mean:

What are the ingredients that make a human being?

and/or

What distinguishes human beings from other animals?

To which she might reply:

Human beings are the most highly evolved animal that we know of. What distinguishes human beings from other animals, as far as we know, are those faculties of the brain which include sentience (self-awareness or consciousness) and the ability to communicate through language and to interact accordingly with nature."

The Religious Believer may interpret the question thus:

What distinguishes human beings from other animals?

and

What is the relationship of humans to God and their ultimate purpose?

To which he might reply:

Human beings are different to other animals because they are SPIRITUAL creatures, made in the image of God. As such, they are self-aware, capable of moral choice and can communicate, through language, with others and the world around them. Their relationship with God is often strained by sin but, through Grace, humans have the right to become "Sons" of God.

Clearly, there are some stark differences as well as areas of common ground. What is meant by the **IMAGE OF GOD (IMAGO DEI)** is particularly interesting and difficult to define.

EVOLUTION

Most people are familiar with evolutionary theories and I will only remind you of the basic premises. There is not enough room in this Study Guide to delve into its various complexities or discuss all strands of evolution (such as evolutionary psychology).

The English naturalist **CHARLES DARWIN** (1809-1882) is, of course, credited with first positing the theory of evolution following the publication of his acclaimed and infamous book, On the Origin of Species by Means of Natural Selection, or the Preservation of Favoured Races in the Struggle for Life, in 1859.

It is perhaps no wonder it caused (and, in some circles, continues to cause) such a stir when, in his introduction, Darwin writes:

> *Although much remains obscure, and will long remain obscure, I can entertain no doubt, after the most deliberate study and dispassionate judgment of which I am capable, that the view which most naturalists entertain, and which I formerly entertained - namely, that each species has been independently created - is erroneous. I am fully convinced that species are not immutable; but that those belonging to what are called the same genera are lineal descendants of some other and generally extinct species, in the same manner as the acknowledged varieties of any one species are the descendants of that species. Furthermore, I am convinced that Natural Selection has been the main but not exclusive means of modification.*

Clearly this challenged the accepted wisdom of the day which (in Victorian England) was largely a Christian, generally literal interpretation of Genesis (as discussed above).

However, it is worth noting two points:

- There is little evidence to suggest that Darwin intended his book as a polemical attack on Christianity or any other religious faith. (In this respect, he is no Dawkins.) Indeed, his wife Emma was supportive of his work despite her Christian (Unitarian) beliefs.

- He did not "start" atheism. Although his publications probably gave rise to a greater apostasy that had been hitherto witnessed, by 1859, the Enlightenment had already taken its toll on religious belief from philosophy and science. The scepticism of David Hume (1711-1776) had paved the way for more forthright agnosticism (often viewed as anti-theism) of Darwin's friend and colleague Thomas Huxley (1825-1895).

The vilification of Charles Darwin by subsequent communities, is therefore, rather unfair. Remember that, above all, scientists work from empiricism and draw their conclusions from what they have observed and measured.

In a nutshell, the theory of evolution rests upon the general observations of:

- the **SURVIVAL OF THE FITTEST** and

- similarity between and within species.

This leads to the development of theories of:

- **NATURAL SELECTION** and **SEXUAL SELECTION** and

- common ancestry and descent.

By looking at **VARIATION** within species, Darwin made several observations. Take the example of household pets - there are hundreds of different dog and cat breeds. Darwin offers a reasonable hypothesis to explain this in the early chapters of Origin, that is that the same animal looking for food in different countries will have different experiences (particularly seasonally), giving rise to the formation of sub-breeds.

Survival of the fittest

Darwin begins his third chapter by remarking that there is a general struggle for existence. He then demonstrates that those animals who are "fittest" - ie best adapted to their environment - will survive AND, "(which is more important) ... succe[ed] in leaving progeny".

Let us suppose there are two bears competing for a single food source. Should it come to a fight, the stronger bear will overcome the other and eat the food. He will then survive and, potentially produce offspring. Even if they are not in direct competition with each other but belong to two different bear communities, the bear who has a stronger constitution is more likely to survive any extreme conditions and thus live to pass its genes on.

This is surely obvious and, in itself, presents no challenge to Religion.

What Darwin does say of survival is:

> [E]ach organic being is striving to increase at a geometrical ratio; that each at some period of its life, during some season of the

year, during each generation or at intervals, has to struggle for life, and to suffer great destruction. When we reflect on this struggle, we may console ourselves with the full belief, that the war of nature is not incessant, that no fear is felt, that death is generally prompt, and that the vigorous, the healthy, and the happy survive and multiply.

The principle of multiplication cannot be underestimated: Evolution is not simply a process of individual survival.

▸ **Compare the meerkats!**

Meerkat 1 - slow and weak

Meerkat 2 - fast and strong

Unfortunately, Meerkat 2 is killed in a freak yachting accident. Meerkat 1 is not and goes on to produce baby meerkats. Thus, the strong genes of Meerkat 2 are not passed on.

Natural selection

The question as to what gives the meerkats their advantage has been developed over time to include genetic mutation. Darwin's general explanation is what he calls "natural selection" (a phrase found some 240 times in Origin).

> *The theory of natural selection is grounded on the belief that each new variety, and ultimately each new species, is produced and maintained by having some advantage over those with which it comes into competition; and the consequent extinction of less-favoured forms almost inevitably follows.*

The current thinking is that genetic **MUTATIONS** randomly occur in all species. Where these are useful, they aid survival and are then passed on to offspring until they become part of that species.

Perhaps this is the answer to "how the leopard got his spots":

> *Once upon a time there was a leopard who was born with a freak mutation - he had spots. Outcast from his family, he wanders about, friendless. However, he finds his "freak" condition enables him to be better camouflaged. This makes him a more successful predator as well as protecting him from other predators. Eventually he meets a nice girl leopard and he passes his useful mutation of spots to their children, who become the dominant leopards ...*

Of course, some mutations are probably unhelpful and these are less likely to be passed down to subsequent generations (although not necessarily - think back to our example of the meerkats). This is because natural selection is, arguably, at the mercy of sexual selection.

Sexual selection

Most teenagers know the pain of trying to "fit in". The mating practices of humans are often harsh. Pressure on men and women to live up to an "ideal" image perpetuated by the media is, arguably, to blame for much misery and a myriad of singletons who, for whatever reason, deem themselves unattractive or to have been "passed over".

One obvious criterion for sexual selection in humans is aesthetics. This has led to heartache and the success of cosmetics companies whose products promise youth and beauty in equal measure. Of course, the old adage that "beauty is in the eye of the beholder" is certainly true to an extent, and so endless debates on Brad Pitt versus Johnny Depp, or Claire Danes versus Beyoncé, ensue. All humans (even twins) are unique and have unique tastes when it comes to what they find sexually attractive.

The other jocular remark that "beauty is in the eye of the beer-holder" actually makes an important evolutionary point: here, it is not the "survival of the fittest" so much as the progeny of the inebriate. It might be possible to argue that men and women who get drunk, have sex and pass on their genes are doing nothing to advance our species - as, if judgement is impaired, there will be no guarantee that their offspring is the product of two of the "strongest" humans.

What of those people who are deemed physically unattractive? Television programmes such as The Undateables might seem diametrically opposed to the idea of "natural" sexual selection but the truth is that human beings do not choose their mates solely on looks.

Intelligence, money, fame, wit and shared interests all play factors. An "ugly" rich man might well marry a woman 40 years his junior.

Suppose, in the stone age, there is a particularly "weak" Homo sapiens who has no aptitude for running or hunting. In fact, she has autism. However, this gives rise to a certain creative genius and she designs a complicated bear trap to snare unwitting creatures. Thus intelligence and what we might deem "disabilities" are simply other forms of the aforementioned mutations in human genetics that aid survival and are then passed down and developed through generations.

In mentioning "creativity" it is worth considering the role of art in sexual selection. The teacher John Keating in the much-loved film Dead Poets Society says that the purpose of language is "to woo women". If (particularly, but by no means only) women are stirred by the arts, then writing a sonnet or playing Rachmaninov is more likely to lead to coitus. In this respect, geniuses such as Shakespeare and Mozart are, perhaps, among the most highly evolved. However, when we look at Mozart's lifespan, the point about surviving long enough to pass on enough of one's genes becomes even more acute. Dying as he did at the age of 35, he had six children by his wife Constanze. However, four died in infancy and the remaining two males did not marry and were childless. Franz Xaver Wolfgang Mozart (Amadeus' youngest child) did become a composer, perhaps supporting the notion that creativity is hereditary, and useful. The English Romantic poet John Keats (1795-1821) was even less lucky - dying of tuberculosis before siring any children.

We shall return to the question of **BEAUTY** and aesthetics in subsequent sections.

Although we have inevitably strayed from Darwin's original observations, it would be prudent to return to what he has to say about sexual selection. It is a term used 18 times in Origin and it is worth reading a good paragraph or two of Darwin's explanation:

> *[Sexual selection] depends, not on a struggle for existence, but on a struggle between the males for possession of the females; the result is not death to the unsuccessful competitor, but few or no offspring. Sexual selection is, therefore, less rigorous than natural selection. Generally, the most vigorous males, those which are best fitted for their places in nature, will leave most progeny. But in many cases, victory will depend not on general vigour, but on having special weapons, confined to the male sex. A hornless stag or spurless cock would have a poor chance of leaving offspring ... male alligators have been described as fighting, bellowing, and whirling round, like Indians in a war-dance, for the possession of the females; male salmons have been seen fighting all day long; male stag-beetles often bear wounds from the huge mandibles of other males. The war is, perhaps, severest between the males of polygamous animals, and these seem oftenest provided with special weapons ...*

> *Amongst birds, the contest is often of a more peaceful character. All those who have attended to the subject, believe that there is the severest rivalry between the males of many species to attract by singing the females.*

The observation about birds is particularly interesting in light of what we have already touched upon concerning creativity and is explored further in subsequent sections.

COMMON ANCESTRY AND DESCENT

[A]ll the species of the same genus are supposed, on my theory, to have descended from a common parent. - Charles Darwin, On the Origin of Species

Phrased as above, this is perhaps one of the less controversial claims of evolution. After all, the literalist interpretation of Genesis would have us all descended from common parents - Adam and Eve. Darwin never claims in Origin that humans have evolved from apes, although the general evolution of humans was clearly inferred by early readers and sparked further debates.

Evidence

The main body of evidence that helped Darwin develop his theories comes from geology - and, more specifically, **FOSSILS**.

FOSSILS (from the Latin "fossilis", meaning "obtained by digging") are remains of animals, plants and other organisms that have been preserved. Ancient civilisations came across fossils but often supposed them to be bones of mythological creatures, such as dragons. Aristotle, Leonado da Vinci and others suggested that they were the remains of living beings and, by Darwin's time, many specimens had been found and dated.

By observing the fossils and dating them, Darwin began to sense a pattern and inferred a regression from modern animals to their common ancestors. Of course, without a complete record, Darwin was forced to speculate, as in the case below:

But to the progenitor of the upland goose and of the frigate-bird, webbed feet no doubt were as useful as they now are to the most aquatic of existing birds. So we may believe that the progenitor of the seal had not a flipper, but a foot with five toes fitted for walking or grasping; and we may further venture to believe that the several bones in the limbs of the monkey, horse, and bat, which have been inherited from a common progenitor, were formerly of more special use to that progenitor, or its progenitors, than they now are to these animals having such widely diversified habits. Therefore we may infer that these several bones might have been acquired through natural selection, subjected formerly, as now, to the several laws of inheritance, reversion, correlation of growth, &c. Hence every detail of structure in every living creature (making some little allowance for the direct action of physical conditions) may be viewed, either as having been of special use to some ancestral form, or as being now of special use to the descendants of this form—either directly, or indirectly through the complex laws of growth.

There are some creationists who explain away the fossil record by suggesting that God put them there to "test" faith, though this opinion is repudiated by most believers for good theological reasons (namely, God is not a "trickster").

Concestors

By the theory of natural selection all living species have been connected with the parent-species of each genus, by differences not greater than we see between the varieties of the same species at the present day; and these parent-species, now generally extinct, have in their turn been similarly connected with more ancient species; and so on backwards, always converging to the common ancestor of each great class.

Although Darwin does not come out and say as much in Origin, it was inferred early on that this might apply to human beings as well. Recent genetic research has suggested that all human beings are descended from a single woman.

In **DAWKINS**'s book, The Ancestor's Tale: A Pilgrimage to the Dawn of Evolution, he explains that a way to solve the problem of finding a "most recent common ancestor" (MRCA) is to use mathematical models. These are deliberately simple. Take a population figure and work backwards to find the base 2 logarithm (ie the number of times you have to multiply 2 by itself to get that number). To get 5,000, you need to multiply 2 by itself about 12.3 times.

This number gives us the timeframe for the mathematical MRCA for that specified population of 5,000, and this becomes the number of generations between the current population and its MRCA. Dawkins calls this "Chang One". However, if you go back further to find Chang One's MRCA, you hit (what Dawkins calls) "Chang Two" at an earlier point in time. Now the rub is that everybody at the time of Chang Two has the potential to either be the ancestor of Chang One (and everyone) or nobody. If we were to use a time machine and travel back to the time of Chang Two, we wouldn't know which member of the population currently living gives birth to the ancestors of Chang One and whose descendants die or which members of the population produce no offspring. Therefore, explains Dawkins, "80% of individuals in any generation will in theory be ancestors of everybody alive in the distant future."

Of course, the fact that humans do not mate at random - that some may have many children, and others few or none; that, often, humans choose mates who are culturally "appropriate" and so forth - highlights a problem with using the mathematical model only. However, it does, in the case of Tasmania (an island isolated for some 13,000 years), demonstrate the difficulty in maintaining a "young earth" hypothesis - there would have had to have been a point at which there was a **CONCESTOR** (common ancestor) before the tribe was isolated.

This model also presents difficulties for Darwinian natural and sexual selection: for if, at any one time, 80% of the population might become universal ancestors, surely that suggests that they are equally "fit" to survive? The criterion of "fitness" is what is in question here: suppose one takes it to be how many children one will have - then a person such as JS Bach, who sired 20 children, will be "fitter" than Handel, who had none, or Mendelssohn, who had five. However, if we take it to mean the total number of descendants that any one person will ever be responsible for, then it would seem that 80% of the population is equally "fit". Moreover, we could not tell, by going backwards in time, whether Bach or Mendelssohn is responsible for more total descendants - only by going forwards in time, until one line completely ends, and then counting up the total descendants could we then say that Mendelssohn or Bach was the "fitter". Here, Dawkins comes to the rescue by qualifying that what makes genes survive in the past (their "fitness") should not be personified as an "intention to reproduce in the future." Yet the conception of innumerable future progeny is nothing new. One only has to think back to the promise God makes to Abraham in Genesis 15:5: "Look toward heaven and count the stars, if you are able to count them ... so shall your descendants be" for "you shall be the ancestor of a multitude of nations. I will make you exceedingly fruitful; and I will make nations of you, and kings shall come from you." (Genesis 17:5-6)

Family trees

There is a common misconception that we inherit genes equally. Although each parent passes half of their genes to their child, if that child produces offspring, the grandchild may inherit a quarter of its paternal grandfather's genes, or none at all.

This, of course explains why it might be that a child with curly hair is born to parents whose parents have had straight hair for several generations.

So, as genes have their own "family tree", geneticists believe they have been able to trace all living humans' family "gene tree" back to a single woman.

Mitochondrial Eve

MITOCHONDRIAL DNA was the earliest significant part of the human genome to be sequenced. It is passed down through the mother only - just as the Y chromosome (which is responsible for a human embryo "becoming" male) is passed through the male line. Mitochondria are "tiny bodies inside cells, relics of once-free bacteria who, probably about 2 billion years ago, took up exclusive residence inside cells where they have been producing, non-sexually by simple division ever since ... mitochondria constitute an independent line of genetic reproduction inside our bodies, unconnected with the main nuclear line which we think of as our 'own' genes." (The Ancestor's Tale)

56

All human beings currently alive may trace their mitochondrial DNA back to a single MCRA, "Eve". Similarly, tracing DNA up the male line from father to father reaches the MRCA "Y-Chromosome Adam".

This obviously excites creationists, but the geneticists are quick to point out that these two ancestors are not a couple and were probably separated by tens of thousands of years. Indeed, most current scholarship suggests that Y-Chromosome Adam is significantly "younger" than Mitochondrial Eve. Dawkins reports that "today's best 'molecular clock' estimates for their respective dates are about 140,000 years ago for Eve and only about 60,000 for Adam".

This does not surprise certain Christian interpreters of the Bible - they point out that the human gene pool is restarted after the Flood in Genesis 6-8. Thus, all men trace their line back to Noah (as his three sons carried his Y chromosome) but Shem, Ham and Japheth and Noah's wives were not related and thus, tracing human mitochondrial DNA back through the female line goes further back to biblical Eve.

Of course, the difference is that Mitochondrial Eve is a title attributed to an MCRA. Dawkins points out that these are liable to change as ethnic groups die out - they leap forward:

> "Adam and Eve are shifting honorific titles, not names of particular individuals. If, tomorrow, the last member of some outlying tribe were to die, the baton of Adam, or of Eve, could abruptly be thrown forward thousands of years."

Moreover, Dawkins is keen to point out, these Adams and Eves did not live in isolation but were members of communities - indeed, they might have been living in close quarters to other "Adams" and "Eves" who also have surviving descendants.

Nevertheless, the point remains that, according to both Darwinian evolutionary theory and the biblical account of creation, human beings have a common ancestor. Perhaps they are not so different after all: science and religion can both agree we are part of the same "family".

Criticisms

Darwin accepted that the geological record was imperfect. Indeed, he devotes the whole of the ninth chapter of Origin to it.

> [W]e continually over-rate the perfection of the geological record, and falsely infer, because certain genera or families have not been found beneath a certain stage, that they did not exist before that stage. We continually forget how large the world is, compared with the area over which our geological formations have been carefully examined; we forget that groups of species may elsewhere have long existed and have slowly multiplied before they invaded the ancient archipelagoes of Europe and of the United States. We do not make due allowance for the enormous intervals of time, which have probably elapsed between our consecutive formations ...

Critics of evolution might well argue that Darwin's theory is largely an inference drawn from the gaps in knowledge. Francis Bacon wrote, "A little philosophy inclineth man's mind to atheism, but depth in philosophy bringeth men's minds about to religion."

Whether or not one accepts this position as fair or reasonable, it is certainly an interesting turning-inside-out of the old "God of the Gaps" argument. Above all, it demonstrates that, due to the epistemological trauma of our unknowing, both Science and Religion must posture hypothesis which go beyond knowledge and have an element of "guesswork".

Of course, Richard Dawkins holds that the difference between religion and science is that when religion comes across a "gap", it stuffs God into it; science, meanwhile, takes it as a challenge to find the answer. This will be discussed later in the chapter on **DESIGN** arguments.

Common ground?

As we have seen in this chapter, both science and religion tend to agree that human beings are related, that the universe is probably finite and that human beings are the "highest" species known to exist (the most "highly evolved" or the "specially created in the image of God").

Perhaps they are not so dissimilar after all. Just as God is the **WHO** behind Creation, so Evolution is the **WHAT** behind our current existence. Both are relayed and received as story. Both become a grand meta-narrative. This will be examined in subsequent chapters.

One fundamental difference (one that Dawkins dislikes) between evolution and creation is that God does not need to use a process. The Pharisees in the ninth chapter of Matthew's Gospel are extremely proud of their **CONCESTOR**, Abraham, and boast to John the Baptist. Yet, he says:

> Do not presume to say to yourselves, "We have Abraham as our ancestor"; for I tell you, God is able from these stones to raise up children to Abraham. (Matthew 3:9)

Whether or not this is hyperbolic rhetoric, the delineation between creation and evolution will always be that creation is ex nihilo. Creation is (although not necessarily) the leap up the mountain, whereas evolution is (to use Dawkins' phrase), the long climb up "Mount Improbable". Of course, many theists suggest that evolution is simply the process or methodology by which He brought creatures into existence. Just because God might be able to create humans from stones, does not mean that He will. Moreover, one should understand this quotation in its proper context: a preacher's polemic against the prideful Pharisees who presume upon God's sovereignty.

KEY TERMS

- **BIG BANG** - Name given to the apparent "explosion" that caused the universe.

- **CONCESTOR** - Common ancestor.

- **CREATION EX NIHILO** - The doctrine that God created everything out of nothing.

- **DEISM** - A belief in a God who is uninvolved with creation.

- **DOCTRINE** - A Church teaching.

- **DOPPLER EFFECT** - What happens to waves when approaching an observer (they get shorter). The sound of a car approaching appears to bend in pitch as a result.

- **EVOLUTION** - The widely held view that living beings gradually adapt to their environment over time and favourable genetic mutations that aid survival add to improvements in DNA.

- **IMAGE OF GOD** - Central Judeo-Christian belief that humans are specially created to reflect God. Often linked to soul/spirit.

- **INFINITE REGRESS** - The ability to go backwards indefinitely.

- **META-NARRATIVE** - A "grand story" that explains truths.

- **MITOCHONDRIAL EVE** - Genetic term for the MRCA we can trace our mitochondria back to. At present, believed to be the genetic "mother" of all humans currently alive today.

- **MOST RECENT COMMON ANCESTOR (MRCA)** - The concestor most recently living that current organisms are descended from.

- **MUTATIONS** - Changes occurring in DNA that might be favourable or unfavourable.

- **NATURAL SELECTION** - The process by which "nature" selects the best. Linked to the survival of the fittest. Whatever helps a living creature survive.

- **RED SHIFT** - A special case of the Doppler effect in the visible light spectrum

- **SEXUAL SELECTION** - Whatever helps a living creature reproduce.

- **SURVIVAL OF THE FITTEST** - One of the axioms of evolutionary theory - the strong survive and the weak do not.

SELF-ASSESSMENT QUESTIONS

1. What is the Big Bang theory?

2. What is the order of creation in Genesis 1?

3. Why does the Big Bang theory present difficulties for creationists?

4. Explain the difference between natural and sexual selection.

5. How would you define humanity?

6. To what extent is evolution compatible with a belief in a Creator God?

7. To what extent does the Big Bang theory aid cosmological arguments for the existence of God?

8. What are the different interpretations of Genesis 1 and 2?

9. "Schools should teach Creation as an alternative to Evolution." What do you think?

10. Write an imaginary debate between Darwin and a Creationist.

Design arguments

For since the creation of the world God's invisible qualities - his eternal power and divine nature - have been clearly seen, being understood from what has been made, so that people are without excuse. - Romans 1:20 (NIV)

Design arguments for the existence of God are **TELEOLOGICAL** (from the Greek "telos", meaning "end"). Design arguments look at the "end product" (the world) and argue backwards from it. (This is not to be confused with cosmological arguments, which were mentioned earlier. "Backwards" does not necessarily mean with reference to causation. The difference is that design arguments still focus on the end product as it is now).

The most famous formulation of the design argument is found in **WILLIAM PALEY**'s work of 1800, entitled Natural Theology or Evidence of the Existence and Attributes of the Deity Collected from the Appearances of Nature.

Paley imagines walking across a heath and finding a stone. There would be no reason not to suppose "it had lain there forever". However, if he were to stumble upon a watch; upon examination of its mechanical workings and the way it looks,

... the inference we think is inevitable, that the watch must have had a maker - that there must have existed, at some time and at some place or other, an artificer or artificers who formed it for the purpose which we find it actually to answer, who comprehended its construction and designed its use.

In the same way, Paley supposes that:

> ... *every observation which was made in our first chapter concerning the watch may be repeated with strict propriety concerning the eye, concerning animals, concerning plants, concerning, indeed, all the organised parts of the works of nature.*

Thus, Paley goes on to argue that the world must have had a designer - that is, a Creator, God.

For Paley, the eye itself is enough to convince him of a Creator. This is, presumably, because the eye is an extremely complex organ. Indeed, supporters of design arguments often use **MICHAEL BEHE**'s phrase Irreducible complexity to describe something that is "composed of several well-matched, interacting parts that contribute to the basic function, wherein the removal of any one of the parts causes the system to effectively cease functioning." (Michael Behe, Darwin's Black Box) If something is indeed irreducibly complex, the argument goes, it cannot have gradually developed but must have been designed in its present form.

Of course, several problems arise from the argument, but the main two are as follows.

Even if the eye had a designer, we cannot tell very much about the designer from the design. Just as we could not tell how many children the watchmaker has from studying the watch - what his or her favourite colour is and even if the watchmaker is still alive, so it is difficult to know things about the designer of the world, even if the general thesis is accepted.

Evolution is offered as an alternative explanation for the eye.

To demonstrate how this might better work, Paley's analogy could be updated thus:

> *Suppose I find an iPhone, while walking in the woods one day. I would not suppose it had always been there. Resisting the urge to immediately eBay the item or simply pocket the device, I examine it. Playing with the phone (assume it has been left unlocked) reveals it responds to touch, tells me things, has different apps and can be used to play music and videos, as well as to take notes. I would assume that it has been designed. When I read on the back of the device "Designed by Apple in California, assembled in China", my suspicions are confirmed.*
>
> *If I had never heard of the company Apple, I might surmise the following:*
>
> *Apple is either a person or persons, whose collective design skills are impressive. Apple is clearly interested in music, video, recreation and productivity. Apple seems to have designed the device for humans to use - as it responds to human touch.*
>
> *However, I cannot tell, simply by studying the phone, anything about Steve Jobs, Jony Ives or any member of the teams of designers. Even Siri will only tell me that "I, Siri, was designed by Apple in California."*
>
> *The components within the iPhone - the computer chips and other hardware, are not irreducibly complex and have not all*

67

been designed by Apple. This particular model I find is one in a series of iPhones, so that, one might say, there is a certain "evolution" at work in creating the current model. This has a fingerprint sensor, but take that away, it would still be an iPhone, though not an iPhone 5S. Take away Siri, the lightning connector and squash the shape and it could be an iPhone 4. It is not, in other words, irreducibly complex.

In the same way, the world could comprise parts designed by other gods or beings. St Paul claims, in the passage above, that there is a sort of "stamp" of divinity on creation, yet the fact that not everybody who looks at the world interprets it as a work of deliberate creation means the "stamp" cannot be self-evident.

The eye

The eyes are considered, by Darwin, to be an example of "organs of extreme perfection and complication", as shown in this quote from On the Origin of Species:

> *To suppose that the eye, with all its inimitable contrivances for adjusting the focus to different distances, for admitting different amounts of light, and for the correction of spherical and chromatic aberration, could have been formed by natural selection, seems, I freely confess, absurd in the highest possible degree. Yet reason tells me, that if numerous gradations from a perfect and complex eye to one very imperfect and simple, each grade being useful to its possessor, can be shown to exist; if further, the eye does vary ever so slightly, and the variations be inherited, which is certainly the case; and if any variation or*

modification in the organ be ever useful to an animal under changing conditions of life, then the difficulty of believing that a perfect and complex eye could be formed by natural selection, though insuperable by our imagination, can hardly be considered real.

Because many proponents of teleological arguments for the existence of God start with the assumption that, if the world had not been designed, it could only have come about by **CHANCE** (which is extremely improbable,) supporters of design arguments (especially irreducible complexity) might hazard that "half an eye" or "half a wing" is no use at all. However, as Dawkins points out, in The God Delusion:

A cataract patient with the lens of her eye surgically removed can't see clear images without glasses, but can see enough not to bump into a tree or fall over a cliff. Half a wing is indeed not as good as a whole wing, but it is certainly better than no wing at all.

The argument espoused further is that, although eyes are currently complex, the "climb up Mount Improbable" (to use Dawkins' metaphor) was probably slow and (so Dawkins believes) the eye evolved slowly over a long period of time from something that simply let light in, to what it is in humans today.

This would seem to be a satisfactory alternative to the design thesis. Dawkins also suggests that:

A deep understanding of Darwinism teaches us to be wary of the easy assumption that design is the only alternative to chance, and teaches us to seek out graded ramps of slowly increasing complexity.

Of course, we need to be similarly wary of Dawkins, who sees everything through the paradigmatic glasses of Darwinian evolution, as a naturalist/ evolutionary biologist.

CHANCE OR DESIGN?

A supporter of design arguments might reason that the Earth is perfectly positioned in proximity to its sun to support life. If we were a fraction closer to the Sun, we should burn; a little farther - we should freeze. Our orbit is near enough circular that we do not stray too far out of the "Goldilocks" zone (neither too hot nor too cold). This is too unlikely to have come about by sheer chance. Rather, the Earth must have been designed so.

Unfortunately, even for those who do believe the Earth has been designed by God, it is far too easy to spot the fallacious logic to this line of reasoning. It is on the same level as telling someone not to play the lottery because "nobody wins", or to call it a "miracle" when someone does. The odds of winning the lottery are extremely improbable, but there is a chance it might happen and, in fact, it does happen. There have even been people who have won it twice, which is incredibly improbable! If we thought that there was a "design" to the lottery, then nobody should play it because no one wants a fixed game of chance. It ceases to be chance. By the same token, the very fact that we are on this planet, questioning our existence and marvelling at the improbability of our existence means that it is **POSSIBLE**. However improbable it is that the right elements should all come together for our planet to sustain life - the creatures who are able to write about it prove that it **CAN** happen and, furthermore, that it did not necessarily have to involve a designer. Note that this counter-argument cannot prove that there **WAS** no designer, merely that it **COULD** have come about without one.

Design is not the only alternative to chance. Natural selection is a better alternative. Indeed, design is not a real alternative at all because it raises an even bigger problem than it solves: who designed the designer? - Dawkins, The God Delusion

Of course, Dawkins falls into the usual trap of asking a question along the lines of "why is a donkey a carrot?" God is believed, by theists, to be infinite, omnipotent and so forth. The watchmaker in Paley's analogy is human, but the designer of the universe is believed to be a being so radically other to us that words will ultimately fail at some level to describe Him. This is where the design argument borrows from Aquinas the language of the Prime Mover or First Cause. As soon as we posit that the designer is the Uncaused Cause, it is a logical absurdity to ask, what caused the Uncaused Caused, on the level of asking why a chair is a giraffe, or a carrot a donkey. Thus, while asking "who designed the designer?" or "who made God?" sounds like a good philosophical question, it is, in fact, absurd when one has understood what the question is really asking.

This highlights, once again, the importance of understanding the question being asked, and the possible differences between Science and Religion, as well as their similarities. Perhaps it is not Dawkins' fault that he falls into the absurd trap as above: for the empiricist, all known designers are contingent beings. It is only with recourse to Philosophy - a discipline which invites the thinker to think beyond the empirical - that such questions can be properly articulated.

ANTHROPIC PRINCIPLE

In Philosophy, the Anthropic Principle is often cited as one that supports design arguments for the existence of God. The Greek word "anthropos" means "man", and the central idea here is that, as the universe supports human life, it must have been designed to do so.

FR TENNANT (1866-1957) is commonly attributed with the development of this Anthropic Principle along two lines:

- The **WEAK** Anthropic Principle points out that if the conditions of the world, solar system and universe were any different, we simply would not be here.

- The **STRONG** Anthropic Principle suggests that the conditions of the universe are only such as to benefit us: ie the design of the universe is anthropocentric (centred on humanity).

However, these distinctions are actually found in Barrow and Tippler's work of 1986, The Anthropic Cosmological Principle. FR Tennant's work on the Anthropic Principle is largely found in the fourth chapter of the second volume of his Philosophical Theology (1930), under the general heading of "The Empirical Approach to Theism: Cosmic Teleology".

Indeed, Tennant is more sophisticated than the "strong" or "weak" anthropic principles cited above. His main thesis is that the "anthropic" and "aesthetic" and "moral" arguments all add weight to **TELEOLOGY** (design arguments). Moreover, teleology is not, for Tennant, incompatible with evolution, as he states in Philosophical Theology:

> ... a teleological interpretation of Nature does not require that every detail in Nature was purposed or fore-ordained. Processes

may inevitably produce by-products which, as such, were not
purposed, but are the necessary outcome of processes by which
a purpose is fulfilled.

More explicitly:

... natural selection is not incompatible with teleology on a
grander scale: as exponents of Darwinism were perhaps the first
to recognise and to proclaim. Subversive of Paley's argument, it
does not invalidate his theistic conclusion, nor even his view that
every organism and organ is an end as well as a means. Indeed
the science of evolution was the primary source of the wider
teleology current for the last half century, as well as the main
incentive to the recovery of the closely connected doctrine of
divine immanence.

Pointing out that "Darwin did not account for the origin of variations;
their forthcomingness was simply a datum for him", Tennant goes on to
suggest that the "discovery of organic evolution has caused the
teleologist to shift his ground from special design in the products to
directivity in the process, and plan in the primary collocations". In
layman's terms, Tennant suggests that evolution could merely be the
process by which God designed the world and its creatures.

His argument then ensues along the following lines:

1. The world is (more or less) intelligible by human beings as a
   COSMOS (an ordered universe) and it is extremely improbable
   that this should be the result of chance.

2. Since Darwinian evolution has not explained what causes
   variation, "gradualness of construction is in itself no proof of the

absence of external design" - ie evolution does not falsify the "God hypothesis".

3. "The fitness of our world to be the home of living beings depends upon certain primary conditions, astronomical, thermal, chemical, etc" and the probability that the "apparent preparedness of the world to be a theatre of life" is simply a matter of chance is "infinitesimally small".

4. The **BEAUTY** of the world is another "link in the chain of evidence". Ultimately, beauty provides no survival value. Rather, it is suggestive of a Creator who delights in beauty.

5. "Natural selection can only explain the emergence and persistence of such moral conduct and principles as possess survival-value for individuals or societies, between which the struggle for existence obtains; and survival-value does not pertain to the higher morality" - ie human morality suggests design and ultimate purpose.

Perhaps the most important point to make here is that, for Tennant, the teleological argument is best understood as a chain of cumulative evidence. Basil Mitchell uses an analogy of a ship, at sea in stormy weather during wartime:

> *In a ship at sea in stormy weather, the officer of the watch reports a lighthouse on a certain bearing. The navigating officer says he cannot have seen a lighthouse, because his reckoning puts him a hundred miles away from the nearest land. He must have seen a waterspouts or a whale blowing or some other marine phenomenon which can be taken for a lighthouse. The officer of the watch is satisfied he must have made a mistake.*

Shortly afterwards, however, the lookout reports land on stop now. The navigating officer, still confident in his working, says it must be cloud - and it is indeed very difficult to distinguish cloud from land in these conditions. But then a second cloud-looking-like-land or land-looking-like-cloud appears on another bearing. It really does begin to look as if the navigator might be out in his reckoning. He has, perhaps, under estimated current, or his last style site was not as good as before it was. The reported sightings are consistent with one another and indicate that he is approaching land.

If it is wartime and the coast is hostile, he had better soon that he is where the sightings placing, and get away from it quickly. It would be nice to be sure that, but in the circumstances it would be prudent to act on the hypothesis which gives him the stronger reason for action. (Basil Mitchell, The Justification of Religious Belief, pp112-113)

Eventually, then, it is the accumulation of evidence that tips the balance. Although this is perfectly reasonable and, arguably, the approach that Darwin himself took, when developing evolutionary theory as the cumulative weight of evidence, the very fact that some will use the same cumulative evidence to draw one conclusion and others, a different conclusion, highlights the flaw with this inductive argument as showing any conclusive "proof" of the teleological (or, indeed, atheistic) thesis. Moreover, just because it is reasonable to draw a conclusion from a chain of cumulative evidence, it doesn't make it true. Mitchell's parable might have had a very different ending. Nevertheless, just as Aquinas's famous "five ways" should be taken cumulatively, so too, Tennant's teleological arguments should be read together. Furthermore, the language Tennant uses is inductive and suggestive. At no point does he claim to prove the existence of God, merely he demonstrates the teleologist's position is not unreasonable and, all things considered, the weight of evidence is decidedly in favour of a designer (God). In the same way, careful readers of Aquinas's Ways in the Summa Theologica will understand them, not as "proofs" for God's existence but ways to demonstrate that belief in God is reasonable - more reasonable than disbelief.

Properly regarded then, Tennant's cosmic teleology is an **ABDUCTIVE** argument.

Deductive, inductive and abductive reasoning

In Deductive arguments, a set of premises or propositions lead to a necessary conclusion, eg:

P1 John is a bachelor.

P2 All bachelors are unmarried men.

C John is an unmarried man.

The argument is valid and sound. The only way to attack it would be to show that John is not a bachelor or that there is a different meaning of the word bachelor.

Inductive arguments, have a set of premises that lead to a likely conclusion. Often, inductive arguments contain a hypothetical (if) and move from general principles to a specific incident, eg:

P1 John is a bachelor.

P2 Most bachelors are unhappy.

C Therefore John is unhappy.

The argument may be valid but it is not sound. It is possible to agree with P1 and P2 and draw a different conclusion - that John is one of the few lucky bachelors who is happy. One might also disagree with either P1 or P2.

As inductive arguments, Abductive arguments do not require their premises to lead to a necessary conclusion. Often described as a "best guess", the inference is drawn from often-incomplete observations. This happens in criminal trials, medical diagnoses and the development of scientific theories as a matter of course. It is often regarded as a more "honest" way of reasoning as within the argument, it concedes that one might be wrong, eg:

P1 I've never seen John with any woman or man.

P2 Many bachelors are unhappy.

P3 John is very often quite miserable. Particularly around couples.

C I think John is a bachelor. I might be wrong, but it would answer a lot of questions.

In Vardy's words (in God Matters), "Abductive reasoning goes beyond what observations can logically support to conclude what seems to be the best explanation for the evidence."

Arguments against the Anthropic Principle

Dawkins turns the whole anthropic project on its head in suggesting (in The God Delusion) that the Anthropic Principle is simply an alternative to the "God hypothesis" or design argument:

> The anthropic principle, like natural selection, is an alternative to the design hypothesis. It provides a rational, design-free explanation for the fact that we find ourselves in a situation propitious to our existence.

However, upon closer inspection, this seems to be just an attempt to hijack a philosophical argument (however sound or unsound) for the existence of God. All Dawkins points out is that, while it is extremely improbable for the conditions to support life to come together, the fact that we are here means it is not impossible:

> It has been estimated that there are between 1 billion and 30 billion planets in our galaxy, and about 100 billion galaxies in the universe. Knocking a few noughts off for reasons of ordinary prudence, a billion billion is a conservative estimate of the number of available planets in the universe. Now, suppose the origin of life, the spontaneous arising of something equivalent to DNA, really was a quite staggeringly improbable event. Suppose it was so improbable as to occur on only one in a billion planets ... even with such absurdly long odds, life will still have arisen on a billion planets - of which Earth, of course, is one.

Again, the only thing that Dawkins demonstrates here is that it is a distinct statistical **POSSIBILITY** that the conditions to support human life should occur within such a vast universe of possible worlds.

It is the same logic that says that an infinite number of monkeys on infinite typewriters would eventually type the complete works of Shakespeare.

One could use the same logic as follows:

P1 There is an infinite number of universes.

P2 It is possible that one of these universes is contingent upon a Necessarily Existent, Supreme, Greatest Conceivable Being.

P3 Therefore a Necessarily Existent, Supreme, Greatest Conceivable Being exists in at least one universe.

P4 A Necessarily Existent, Supreme, Greatest Conceivable Being who exists in all universes is more maximally great than one who exists in only one universe.

C Therefore a Necessarily Existent, Supreme, Greatest Conceivable Being exists in all universes.

Something like this has already been proposed by Swinburne and is, of course, critiqued by atheists - perhaps rightly so - for simply arguing God into existence from sheer probability. Yet this is precisely the same line of reasoning as Dawkins employs above: Just because there is a statistical possibility that, given the number of planets in existence, one of them should develop human life, does not mean that it **MUST** have been designed so, **NOR** that it **CANNOT** have been designed. It is very easy for Dawkins to simply assert that the Anthropic Principle is an alternative explanation to the design argument for the existence of human life, but it is simply that he has decided to call the theory of statistical probability by the same name as a genuine (however convincing or weak) argument for the existence of God, and philosophers would do well to be aware of such arbitrary (or possibly calculated) designations by Dawkins and his ilk which are, essentially rhetorical devices and not genuine arguments.

THE AESTHETIC PRINCIPLE

Also known as the argument from beauty, this was also developed by Tennant in the second volume of his Philosophical Theology and can be summarised as follows:

P1 The world is beautiful.

P2 The world does not need to be beautiful to aid survival in a Darwinian framework.

C The world has been purposely designed to be beautiful.

Two obvious lines of criticism immediately present themselves:

- "Beauty" is subjective ("in the eye of the beholder").

- It would seem that beauty is useful in the struggle to survive.

"Beauty is subjective"

David Hume (in Essays: Moral, Political and Literary) observed that:

> Beauty is no quality in things themselves: It exists merely in the mind which contemplates them; and each mind perceives a different beauty. One person may even perceive deformity, where another is sensible of beauty.

This might seem to immediately deflate the theist's premise: the world is only perceived to be beautiful - in reality, it is neither beautiful nor ugly, because beauty requires an observer.

The word "merely" is, arguably, the clincher and, as such, the moot point. Take out the word "merely" and we see that, while attributing beauty to an object or person is certainly, to some degree, a matter of opinion, the fact that we are using the word "beauty" suggests that it exists, as a concept, within the minds of all people. This is the idea of beauty. In other words, although we might differ on what constitutes beauty ("gentlemen prefer blondes", and there's no accounting for taste), this does not mean that the basic concept of beauty is not, to some degree, universal. What people argue over are particular instances of beauty.

In a similar way, it is difficult to define a colour but easy to point to objects that are yellow, blue, red and so forth. Imagine the following conversation:

Person A: Look at that beautiful red rose!
Person B: That's hardly red. It's pink!
Person C: I'd say it's more like orange!
Person A: It's not orange, there's no yellow in it!
Person B: It's too light in hue to call it "red".
Person C: All right, if it's not orange, how about peach or salmon?

Each person argues as to the shade of the rose, yet none of them claims it is blue; rather, they differ about its redness, according to where they place the somewhat arbitrary English definitions of shade, along the visible light spectrum. The argument can only ensue because all the participants make recourse to the same visible light spectrum.

Apply this to beauty:

Person A:	Audrey Hepburn is beautiful!
Person B:	No, she's too thin. Marilyn Monroe was a real woman.
Person C:	Yeah, I prefer blondes as a rule but Marilyn had that weird "beauty spot" going on.
Person A:	Are you telling me that if Audrey Hepburn or Susan Boyle asked you out on a date, you'd accept Susan Boyle's invitation and not Audrey Hepburn's?
Person B:	That's just silly.
Person A:	Why?
Person C:	Susan Boyle's ugly!
Person B:	I agree.
Person A:	So do I. Then you agree that Audrey Hepburn isn't ugly?
Person C:	I didn't say she was ugly, I just don't think she's particularly beautiful.
Person B:	Right. She's not my type.
Person A:	So who do you think is beautiful?
Person B:	Michelle Pfeiffer.
Person C:	Too old! Megan Fox.
Person A:	Too young!
Person C:	Well, Audrey Hepburn's dead!
Person B:	Michelle Pfeiffer's not too old for me.

Do couples cease to think of their spouse as beautiful after 40 years of marriage? Is that why certain women are worried their husbands will "trade them in for a younger model"? An old woman of 80 is almost certainly not as aesthetically pleasing as she was in her twenties or thirties, yet to the beloved, may still retain that beauty because of the love borne for her. Thus, beauty is more than "skin deep". Moreover, there are many couples who do remain faithful to each other long into their old age. This is not because the husband does not see young women of twenty-something as "beautiful" in comparison; it is possible to retain an intellectual appreciation of a person or object as being aesthetically pleasing, while not desiring them. Similarly, heterosexual women may agree that a female of their acquaintance is "beautiful" without having any desire for her. Thus, we begin to see that the appreciation of beauty is not limited to biology and not "merely" in the mind which contemplates objects of beauty, but in the collective conscious as an intellectual standard, by which instances of beauty are measured.

As Keats famously wrote, in "Ode on a Grecian Urn":

> ... beauty is truth, truth beauty - that is all /
> Ye know on earth, and all ye need to know.

This is of course a Romantic proposition, but it resonates with FD Schleiermacher's Feeling of Absolute Dependence (in The Christian Faith), whereby all humans have an immediate experience of the Divine.

The 18th C is not only where we find Paley and Hume, but also Wordsworth. As the Enlightenment gave rise to increasing faith in the powers of empiricism to solve the epistemological traumas of our ignorance, so too the greatest poets became convinced that the locus of human knowledge was not in our ratio (the rational mind, or science) but in Feeling:

> Books! 'tis a dull and endless strife:
> Come, hear the woodland linnet,
> How sweet his music! on my life,
> There's more of wisdom in it.

And hark! how blithe the throstle sings!
He, too, is no mean preacher:
Come forth into the light of things,
Let Nature be your teacher.

She has a world of ready wealth,
Our minds and hearts to bless -
Spontaneous wisdom breathed by health,
Truth breathed by cheerfulness.

One impulse from a vernal wood
May teach you more of man,
Of moral evil and of good,
Than all the sages can.

Sweet is the lore which Nature brings;
Our meddling intellect
Mis-shapes the beauteous forms of things: -
We murder to dissect.

Enough of Science and of Art;
Close up those barren leaves;
Come forth, and bring with you a heart
That watches and receives.

In another of his Lyrical Ballads, he writes:

Love, now a universal birth,
From heart to heart is stealing,

From earth to man, from man to earth:
- It is the hour of feeling.

One moment now may give us more
Than years of toiling reason:
Our minds shall drink at every pore
The spirit of the season.

The primacy of feeling is not "mere" intuition or emotion, but a real and immediate dialogue with the natural world and it is this rapport between humanity and Nature which, for Tennant, is so indicative of an ordered cosmos, designed to be intelligible:

Nature's potency to evoke aesthetic sentiment, however otiose in the cosmic process studied by science, is efficient in the world's rapport with man.

Again, he argues that the intelligibility of our world which might have well been simply a chaos has yet to be explained by atheistic philosophy.

Wordsworth, Keats and Socrates would all agree with Tennyson's succinct observation that "we cannot know, we have but faith / for knowledge is of things we see". For the beginning of true wisdom is an admission of ignorance. The epistemological implications and how they impact on the general debate between Science and Religion will be discussed in the last chapter.

Whether or not beauty is truly subjective, most would agree with Tennant that:

[O]n the telescopic and on the microscopic scale, from the starry heaven to the siliceous skeleton of the diatom, in her inward

parts ... as well as on the surface, in flowers that "blush unseen" and gems that the "unfathomed caves of ocean bear", Nature is sublime or beautiful, and the exceptions do but prove the rule. However various be the taste for beauty, and however diverse the levels of its education or the degrees of its refinement, Nature elicits aesthetic sentiment from men severally and collectively; and the more fastidious becomes this taste, the more poignantly and the more lavishly does she gratify it.

The key here is that "Nature elicits aesthetic sentiment". It is this universality that suggests, for Tennant, something comparable to the uniformity of natural law, to such an extent that he writes:

That natural Objects evoke aesthetic sentiment is as much a fact about them as that they obey the laws of motion or that they have such and such chemical composition.

Just because people may differ about what is beautiful, does not mean there is no objective beauty. Indeed, it rather suggests there must be some ontal Form (to borrow from Plato) of beauty, or else there would be no point in arguing over it. Dawkins would be one of the first to wax lyrical about the beauty of the world.

It would seem that beauty is useful in the struggle to survive

Karl Grammer et al (in Biology Review, 2003) assert that, in humans:

> *Female beauty signals youth, fertility and health while male resources signal male competitive ability and health.*

For teleologists, this remark is reductive.

It is almost certainly indisputable that, in the animal kingdom, beauty aids sexual selection and, thus, survival. From the feathers of a peacock to the "fearful symmetry" of a tiger (William Blake, "The Tyger"), many creatures' aesthetics make them attractive to prospective mates.

Darwin observed that:

> *[T]he rock-thrush of Guiana, birds of Paradise, and some others, congregate; and successive males display their gorgeous plumage and perform strange antics before the females, which standing by as spectators, at last choose the most attractive partner.*

However, even among the birds, what is regarded as beautiful is sometimes arbitrary or subjective, and he reports that "Sir R Heron has described how one pied peacock was eminently attractive to all his hen birds."

Thus, even the subjective nature of beauty is useful, as it "gives people a chance".

Groups of teenagers (particuarly, perhaps, those who follow the American trends) often "rate" members of the opposite sex on a scale of 1 to 10 and perpetuate a social myth that you can only date within 1 or 2 of where you lie on the scale. So if a boy is deemed by his friends to be a "6", he should be looking to date women who are between 5 and 7 on the scale. Although this has the illusion of standardising, or objectifying, beauty, the reality is that the scale is arbitrary. What matters is not where the boy's friends place him on the scale, but where the intended date does. Moreover, self-image/esteem is bound to play a significant psychological role and it might be argued that if a boy thinks of himself of being "worthy" of a woman, his confidence will help (or hinder) him.

Of course, he is commended by his friends if he manages to date someone "out of his league" but, if the scale were truly objective and he were a "3", and the girl a "9", then one might wonder why the girl was prepared to date him.

Perhaps because, in humans, sexual selection is not only based on aesthetics.

The following dialogue from the 1986 film When Harry Met Sally is illuminating:

> Jess: You're saying that she's not that attractive.
>
> Harry: No, I told you she is attractive.
>
> Jess: Yeah, but you also said she had a good personality.
>
> Harry: She has a good personality. What?
>
> Jess: When someone's not that attractive, they're always described as having a good personality.

Harry: Look, if you'd asked me, "What does she look like?" and I said, "She has a good personality", that means she's not attractive, but just because I happen to mention that she has a good personality, she could be either: she could be attractive with a good personality or not attractive with a good personality.

Jess: What is she?

Harry: Attractive.

Jess: But not beautiful, right?"

The ideal human sexual behavioural model that prevails in modern Western societies seems to be monogamy, or serial monogamy - ie, humans select mates, or partners, with whom they form (mainly) exclusive relationships. If that ends through death or because one or both of the couple no longer wish to be in the relationship, many will pursue future relationships; often with the hope of finding "the one" with whom they can grow old together. Thus, when selecting mates, humans might consider personality, economic status, intelligence, sense of humour, similarity of interests, religious or political opinions and so forth. Bill Nighy's character in Richard Curtis' 2013 film About Time has this piece of advice to give on his son's wedding day: "I'd only give one piece of advice to anyone marrying. We're all quite similar in the end. We all get old and tell the same tales too many times. But try and marry someone kind."

Perhaps this is because, as the writer of Proverbs remarks, "Charm is deceptive, and beauty is fleeting." Much poetry contains the sentiment that youth and beauty fade away, and Shakespeare's famous Sonnet 18 declares:

> *... Every fair from fair sometime declines,*
> *By chance, or nature's changing course, untrimmed.*

Thus, although beauty is certainly helpful, and arguably the primary contributing factor in sexual selection, it is not the only criterion considered when humans choose mates. Furthermore, the utility of beauty as regards sexual selection neither precludes a designer, nor provides a satisfactory explanation for the prevalence of beauty in the natural world that has very little (if anything) to do with natural and sexual selection, and philosophers should be very wary of evolutionists who might attempt to argue along such lines as it smacks of a **BLIK** about evolution - whereby everything has to be explained through that paradigm.

For example, most people would accept that sunrises and sunsets are beautiful. There seems to be no need for this - no survival value. People who stared at sunsets in the Stone Age well may have left themselves vulnerable to attack; driving a car into a sunset is dangerous. Perhaps the ability to versify about sunsets benefits the poet in terms of sexual selection, if we accept John Keating's observation in Dead Poets Society (1989, Peter Weir) that language was formed for "one endeavour ... to woo women!" then poetry simply becomes another display of sexual prowess, along the lines of the peacock's feathers. However, this does not seem in keeping with what we know of men like John Keats, whose epitaph "here lies one whose name was writ in water" was written by himself in a moment of despair, thinking himself a failure. The great love of his life, Fanny Brawne, did not marry him - possibly because he was deemed too poor by her, her family or Keats himself - and she has come in for vast amounts of criticism by literary scholars for being something of a tease.

Yet, when we read his poetry, lines such as

When I behold, upon the night-starred face,
huge cloudy symbols of a high romance
And think that I may never live to trace
Their shadows with the magic hand of chance

speak to the souls of men (and women).

Poetry, music, art and so forth are surely the human response to the beauty of the natural world, as well as the struggle of and for life and its hidden purpose(s) (if any).

Again, Robin Williams' character from Dead Poets Society muses:

We read and write poetry because we are members of the human race. And the human race is filled with passion. And medicine, law, business, engineering, these are noble pursuits and necessary to sustain life. But poetry, beauty, romance, love; these are what we stay alive for. To quote from Whitman, "O me! O life! ... of the questions of these recurring; of the endless trains of the faithless ... of cities filled with the foolish; what good amid these, O me, O life?" Answer. That you are here - that life exists, and identity; that the powerful play goes on and you may contribute a verse. That the powerful play *goes on* and you may contribute a verse. What will your verse be?

Dawkins marvels at the beauty of the world - indeed, the cosmos. He often criticises religious believers for not marvelling at the beauty of the universe enough. Allying himself with Carl Sagan, Dawkins seems to think that religious believers make God "little" and deny the true grandeur of the universe - presumably by keeping a focus on the known world. This assertion does not ring true for most religious believers and the focus on the known world in the Abrahamic faiths is almost certainly down to a lack of scientific knowledge about the universe and not to an anthropocentric closed-mindedness.

Darwin closes his Origin of Species with the following words:

> [W]hilst this planet has gone cycling on according to the fixed law of gravity, from so simple a beginning endless forms most beautiful and most wonderful have been, and are being, evolved.

Telelogists would not disagree (even if some disagree with the word "evolved"). However, Tennant's Aesthetic Principle goes further in attempting to answer the question as to the ultimate purpose for this beauty:

> If Nature's beauty embody a purpose of God, it would seem to be a purpose for man.

KEY TERMS

- **ABDUCTIVE** - Closely linked to "guessing", this is the sort of reasoning that draws a hypothesis from often inconclusive data.

- **AESTHETIC PRINCIPLE** - Argument for the existence of God based on beauty; ie that the world doesn't have to be beautiful but is designed that way.

- **ANALOGY** - Drawing on familiar objects/situations to demonstrate a similar instance that is not as familiar. Close to metaphors/similes, eg Jesus' parables.

- **ANTHROPIC PRINCIPLE** - The belief that the universe/world has been specifically designed for humans. (From the Greek anthropos = man.)

- **DEDUCTIVE** - Reasoning where a set of propositions lead to a decisive conclusion. If the propositions hold, the conclusion must, also.

- **DESIGN** - The belief that God (or some supernatural agent) has intentionally created the world.

- **FEELING OF ABSOLUTE DEPENDENCE** - Schleiermacher's own term to describe an ineffable, immutable, immediate experience everyone has of the Divine in our sense of being utterly dependent.

- **INDUCTIVE** - Reasoning where the propositions lead to a most likely conclusion. The propositions may be agreed but the conclusion rejected in an inductive argument.

- **IRREDUCIBLE COMPLEXITY** - Something is said to be "irreducibly complex" if, by removing one of its components, it ceases to function completely as that thing.

- **TELEOLOGICAL** - From the Greek "telos" (end), teleological arguments and ethical theories both look to the end product. In philosophy, teleology looks at the end result, ie world, and extrapolates a designer. The "design argument" is a simpler name for teleological arguments for the existence of God.

SELF-ASSESSMENT QUESTIONS

1. What is Paley's form of the design argument?

2. What are the problems with Paley's analogy?

3. Explain the term "irreducible complexity", and why it is important for creationists.

4. Why do you think Dawkins calls Paley's watchmaker "blind"?

5. Is chance the only alternative to design?

6. "Design arguments for the existence of God are the least convincing to atheists but most convincing to theists." Discuss.

7. Outline the Anthropic Principle.

8. How far would you agree that beauty is "only in the eye of the beholder"?

9. To what extent is "abductive reasoning" a useful category in teleological debates?

10. List everything about the world you find beautiful, and determine its "survival value" in a Darwinian framework.

Miracles

WHAT IS A MIRACLE?

The word "miracle" is widely used in modern vernacular to describe any fortunate event. Newspapers are full of stories that propagate the word as a hyperbolic exclamation of good news or an unlikely event. On 26 March 2014, footballer Sol Campbell was quoted as remarking that "A miracle has to happen [for Arsenal to win the league], for the other teams to lose games, for them to win games, for it to all change around." In other news from the same week, a family in Torquay celebrated the first birthday of their "miracle baby Isla" who, despite being "the sickest baby in Britain" had, thankfully, defied the odds of survival. Meanwhile, The Salisbury Post had an article about a captain who "miraculously landed his disabled US Airways jetliner on the Hudson River" in 2009. All 155 aboard survived and one of the passengers, Dave Sanderson, had been speaking in public. The article reported that "one elderly woman told [Sanderson] after his first talk that 'Now I believe there is a God, who performs miracles.'"

Clearly, before any further discussion can take place, the term **MIRACLE** needs to be defined.

Miracles are NOT merely "fortunate" events; nor are they merely "inexplicable" or "improbable" events. Winning the lottery is not a miracle - it is a statistical improbability for any one person, yet considering the number of people who play each week and the finite (even if very great) possible combinations of winning numbers, it is quite likely that someone will win.

Neither does invoking the word "miracle" make something that cannot currently be explained by empiricism an act of God or divine agent.

David Hume's definition is still among the most useful. In An Enquiry Concerning Human Understanding, he defines a miracle as "a transgression of a law of nature" by a particular volition of the Deity, or by the interposition of some invisible agent."

This definition immediately begs the question: "What are the laws of nature?"

Other definitions are looser and are bound up with the interpretation of the event - as in RF Holland's observation that "a coincidence can be taken religiously as a sign and called a miracle" (quoted in Larmer, The Legitimacy of a Miracle).

This notion of miracle is closely linked to religious experience and means that if the experience believes an event (natural, coincidental or supernatural) to be evidence of divine intervention, it can properly be regarded as a miracle.

Quentin Tarantino's 1994 film Pulp Fiction has an excellent example of this sort of anti-realist approach to miracles.

Vincent (John Travolta) and Jules (Samuel L Jackson) are two hitmen who are unharmed when a man opens fire at them at point blank range and misses. Jules immediately calls this "divine intervention" and decides to change his life as a result. Later at a café they have the following conversation:

JULES: I just been sittin' here thinkin'.

VINCENT: About what?

JULES: The miracle we witnessed.

VINCENT: The miracle you witnessed. I witnessed a freak occurrence.

JULES: Do you know what a miracle is?

VINCENT: An act of God.

JULES: What's an act of God?

VINCENT: I guess it's when God makes the impossible possible. And I'm
            sorry Jules, but I don't think what happened this morning
            qualifies.

JULES: Don't you see, Vince, that shit don't matter. You're judging
            this thing the wrong way. It's not about what. It could be God
            stopped the bullets, he changed Coke into Pepsi, he found my
            fuckin' car keys. You don't judge shit like this based on merit.
            Whether or not what we experienced was an according-to-
            Hoyle miracle is insignificant. What is significant is I felt God's
            touch; God got involved.

VINCENT: But why?

JULES: That's what's fuckin' wit' me! I don't know why. But I can't
            go back to sleep.

VINCENT: So you're serious, you're really gonna quit?

JULES: The life, most definitely.

Importantly, Tarantino allows the viewers to draw their own conclusions as to whether the bullets were supernaturally prevented from killing Jules and Vincent. The significance of the event is how it affects the characters, and this is just the sort of approach that German theologian Rudolf Bultmann (1884-1976) takes in his attempt to de-mythologise (ie take out all the "magic" or "supernatural" qualities from) Christianity. Ultimately, Bultmann concludes, the Resurrection was not an event in the life of Jesus but an event in the life of His disciples - a "spiritual reality" as opposed to a historic one.

It should be noted that while this view might sound appealing for liberal theologians wishing to reconcile faith with science, it is completely unsatisfactory for most confessing Christians and decried as heresy by most. Karl Barth, a Swiss contemporary of Bultmann, emphatically argues in favour of the Resurrection's historicity as well as its spiritual significance. (As the central "miracle" of the Christian faith, the Resurrection will be discussed in further detail later.)

Similarly, Hume makes an important distinction between events that are not perceived to be miracles but really are:

Sometimes an event may not, in itself, seem to be contrary to the laws of nature, and yet, if it were real, it might, by reason of some circumstances, be denominated a miracle; because, in fact, it is contrary to these laws. Thus if a person, claiming a divine authority, should command a sick person to be well, a healthful man to fall down dead, the clouds to pour rain, the winds to blow, in short, should order many natural events, which immediately follow upon his command; these might justly be esteemed miracles, because they are really, in this case, contrary to the laws of nature.

Aquinas points out, in Summa Theologica, that "The word miracle is derived from admiration, which arises when an effect is manifest, whereas its cause is hidden."

However, Aquinas is careful to qualify that the hiddenness of the cause, if to be regarded properly as a miracle, must be God - for there are many things whose causes remain "hidden" or unknown to some. A magician's illusions are "hidden" from most of his audience. The example Aquinas uses is that of an eclipse – the cause of which may be hidden to a "rustic" but not to an astronomer. Thus, "a miracle is so called as being full of wonder; as having a cause absolutely hidden from all: and this cause is God. Wherefore those things which God does outside those causes which we know, are called miracles."

The Synoptic Gospels (Mark, Matthew and Luke) use the word "dunamis" to refer to Jesus' miracles as "deeds of power" or "marvellous works". John's Gospel, on the other hand, uses the word "semeion" to denote Jesus' miracles as "signs".

For the purposes of the rest of this section, we shall take miracle to mean an event caused by God (or by divine provenance, through other agents) that contradicts the laws of nature.

THE PHILOSOPHICAL PROBLEM

Two questions immediately present themselves:

1. **CAN** God perform miracles?

2. **DOES** God perform miracles?

If God can, it does not necessarily follow that He does, yet if He does, it must be concluded that He can. This is where Science and Philosophy depart: for the nature of Science is such that it will answer the question **A POSTERIORI**, mainly by establishing an answer to Q2 – whereas Philosophy can make an **A PRIORI** case for or against Q1. Theology, of course, answers Q1 a priori and Q2 a posteriori.

In order to elucidate the apparent dichotomy, each question shall be examined in turn.

CAN GOD PERFORM MIRACLES?

There is a fairly short answer to this question – if God is the author of Nature, then He can supersede it; in much the same way as a computer programmer can alter the parameters of her computer program. However, there is a slightly knottier version of the question which highlights the philosophical difficulty which points out that miracles occur in time, and God is eternal and infinite (outside time), raising the following question.

"Can an eternal God act in time?"

The philosophical problem appears to be: "Can what is radically other to and without something affect something in it? Or can it do so only from the outside?" The analogy of a person throwing stones into a lake might here be drawn: The person, remaining always on the bank, throws stones into the water and causes ripples. She affects the nature of the pond even though she does not become subject to it - she does not even go into it. This is one way we might interpret the question. The second is that the person goes INTO the lake and thus affects it. And of course, the Christian believes this is what God does - He goes into the lake, He parts the Red Sea, He walks on the water, is baptised in the Jordan - the Eternal God, "goes into the Far Country". Yet this is simply to answer the question a posteriori and the task here is to establish the answer a priori.

In order to do this, it would become a primary necessity to revisit our understanding of time. Unfortunately there is not enough room in this Study Guide to do this, but you can find a section on it in the Study Guide on God and Evil.

DOES GOD PERFORM MIRACLES?

In arguments for and against miracles, the question of the "burden of proof" always rears its head: should the burden of proof lie with the empiricist to falsify the miracle, or the believer trying to establish it?

It is obvious that, in order to answer the question, it becomes helpful to either falsify **EVERY** miracle story or **VERIFY** one. (Revisit the Falsification Principle in the earlier chapter and you will see that, much like the green and red apples, if it can be demonstrated that one miracle has occurred, it would falsify the hypothesis that "God does not perform miracles". However, to falsify the hypothesis "God does perform miracles", every "miracle" would have to be falsified in turn, which is impractical.)

Since not every one believes in miracles and there have been several thousand years of claims, it would seem impossible to falsify either hypothesis. However, by examining a few significant miracle stories, we can see how Science and Religion battle it out.

The "Resurrection"

> Now it is no accident that for us the Virgin birth is paralleled by the miracle of which the Easter witness speaks, the miracle of the empty tomb. These two miracles belong together. (Barth, CD p182)

So writes Barth and so it is that, as the central tenet of the Christian faith (possibly preceding, historically, the Virgin birth), the miracle of the Resurrection should be given some space here:

The Nicene Creed affirms belief that Jesus Christ "suffered under Pontius Pilate, was crucified, dead and buried. On the third day, He rose again, in accordance with the scriptures."

"Evidence"	Source
Jesus is crucified and dies	*Matthew 27:45-50, Mark 15:33-37, Luke 23:44-46, John 19:28-30*
Joseph of Arimathea and Nicodemus prepare Jesus' body	*Matthew 27:57-61, Mark 15:42-47, Luke 23:50-56, John 19:31-42*
Women see where Jesus is buried	*Matthew 27:61, Mark 15:47, Luke 23:55*
Guard set	*Matthew 27:62-65,*
Women come to the tomb on Sunday morning	*Matthew 28:1, Mark 16:1, Luke 24:1, John 20:1*
Stone rolled away (described)	*Matthew 28:2-4*
Stone had been rolled away	*Mark 16:4, Mark 16:4 Luke 24:2, John 20:1*
Body of Jesus missing	*Matthew 28:6, Mark16:6, Luke 24:3, John 20:2-7*
Women see angel(s)	*Matthew 28:5-7 (one angel), Mark 16:5-7, Luke 24:4-8*
Women go to tell disciples	*Matthew 28:8, Luke 24:9,*
Peter and John rush to the tomb	*Luke 24:9-12, John 20:2-10*
Jesus appears to Mary Magdalene	*John 20:11-18, [Mark 16:9-11. From the later addition of Mark]*

"Evidence"	Source
Jesus appears to other women	Matthew 28:9-19
Guards' report	Matthew 28:11-15
Jesus appears on the road to Emmaus	Luke 24:13-32
Jesus appears to Peter	Luke 24:33-34, 1 Corinthians 15:5
Jesus appears in the upper room to disciples	Luke 24:36-43, John 20:19-23 [Mark 16:14. From the later addition of Mark]
Jesus appears in the upper room with Thomas	John 20:26-31, 1 Corinthians 15:5 (inferred)
Jesus appears to seven disciples on the beach. Miraculous catch of 153 fish	John 21:1-25
Jesus appears to 500 others	1 Corinthians 15:6
Jesus appears to James	1 Corinthians 15:7
Jesus ascends to heaven	Matthew Luke 24:50-51, Acts 1:9-11
Presupposition of Easter faith/other mentions of the resurrection of Jesus	1 Corinthians 15:1-58, 1 Peter 1:3, Romans 10:9, Acts 17:31, Romans 8:11, Romans 6:4, 1 John 3:2, Romans 8:34, Romans 1:4, 1 Peter 3:18, 1 Thessalonians 4:14, Colossians 1:18, Ephesians 1:20, Galatians 1:1, 2 Corinthians 4:14, Acts 2:24; 31, Acts 3:15, 2 Timothy 2:8, Philippians 3:10, etc.

Unlike the Virgin birth, the Resurrection is attested to by all four gospels and in some letters of the New Testament. The biblical evidence for the Resurrection is, therefore, as follows:

Although not all the elements are present in each source, the key components seem corroborated. The question is, whether this satisfies the historical warrant of multiple attestation (ie if several different sources say the same, or similar things, it is more credible and, perhaps, likely to be true). The answer will largely depend upon one's view of the Bible.

Some obvious **ARGUMENTS AGAINST** the "miracle" of the Resurrection are as follows:

1. It's impossible. Dead is dead!

2. The women got the wrong tomb.

3. The disciples/others stole the body.

4. Jesus didn't really die.

5. The disciples were hallucinating.

6. There are too many inconsistencies with the texts.

7. They're all from the same source.

8. There is no eye-witness account of the resurrection itself.

9. There is a paucity of empirical evidence.

To take each in turn:

1. It's impossible. Dead is dead!

This, as above with the Virgin birth, is precisely what makes it a miracle for believers. Precedents in the Bible for people coming back to life are found in both the Old and New Testaments (Elijah and the widow's son in 1 Kings 17:7-24, Jesus and Lazarus in John 11, etc) but what distinguishes those miracles from the resurrection of Jesus is that the others were only resuscitations: Jairus' daughter, the widows' sons at Zarephath and Nain, Eutychus falling out of the window and the others subsequently died again. Jesus' resurrection is distinctive in that his new resurrected body had "gone through death" and was not subject to the laws of nature. For example, He could walk through walls but also eat.

Once again, denying the Resurrection on the grounds that it's "impossible" is tantamount to saying Michael Bublé's next album will be rubbish. It might be awful, but the claim is only made on a presupposition.

2. The women got the wrong tomb.

This is a distinct possibility and difficult to falsify. Although the gospels tell us that the women saw where Jesus was lain and that two respectable Jews helped bury Jesus, proponents of this view might suggest that, in their heightened emotional state and in the chaos of grief and the confused rush of Passover, the women simply got it wrong. However, it should be noted that the empty tomb is not the only "evidence" given for the Resurrection - the appearances of Jesus afterwards are also taken as evidence for the believers and so this particular criticism can only serve as a link in the chain.

3. The disciples/others stole the body.

This is probably the most popular reductionist explanation for the Resurrection or empty tomb, and was clearly a theory as early as the gospel of Matthew who writes that the chief priests bribed the guards to say that the disciples stole the body while they slept.

Against this, the following might be argued:

As the disciples had all forsaken Jesus following his arrest, except John, who stood at the foot of the cross, it seems unlikely that, the following day, they all got together and stole the body under the noses of the guard. It is incredibly improbable that the soldiers actually had fallen asleep, as penalties would have been severe. The counter-criticism that there never were any guards does not hold in the face of reports circulated that account for the guards missing the stealing of the body, and would have been easily refuted at the time.

It could not be the case that only some of the disciples stole the body, as all claimed to have seen Jesus afterwards. They went from locking themselves in a room, for "fear of the Jewish leaders" to running out into the streets and telling people Jesus was alive again; risking (and in most cases, eventually losing) their lives to spread this "good news". It was unlikely to think anyone would believe them and more probable they would have been severely punished. Their faith in the Resurrection is most likely genuine.

It is equally, if not, more, improbable that the body was stolen by people other than Jesus' disciples - such as grave robbers. Not only would they have needed to roll away the stone and subdue the guards, but what could have been their motive? Jesus was not buried with any earthly goods and the shroud He was wrapped in was left behind. The only thing to disappear was the body, but why take the body? Perhaps the intention was to hold the body to ransom - hoping that the disciples/Jesus' relatives would want to pay to have it back - but there is no evidence of such a ransom demand. Also, in a Jewish community, touching the dead would have rendered them ceremonially unclean and it was still the Feast of the Passover.

The mystery of the empty tomb is a historical mystery as much as anything else, and may never be solved. It was falsifiable at the time and, given the lengths the chief priests went to to have Jesus executed, it would not be a leap to suppose they might have conducted an investigation to locate the body. Rest assured, if they had been able to produce the body, or prove it had been stolen, or that the wrong tomb had been visited on that first day of the week, they would have, and there would be no Christianity today. It is entirely possible that the body was stolen, of course, but there is little empirical evidence for it and if the miracle is to be disproved on empirical grounds, this might not be the best line of enquiry.

4. Jesus didn't really die.

As Barth reports, "even the great [18th-C theologian] Schleiermacher took this view - that Jesus may have come round from an apparent death". This is quite amusing really - it surely takes more "faith" to believe that a man, having been severely beaten and whipped, who was too weak to carry his own cross, who was nailed to a scaffold for three hours, in the presence of witnesses, whose side was pierced, spilling coagulated blood (the separation of plasma seen as "blood and water" - which signified, for the trained Roman soldiers, a confirmation of his death) who was subsequently buried - "came around" from it some hours later and, with such an adrenalin rush, was able to push open his tomb, having stripped off his grave clothes and folded them neatly and run past the guards naked and unnoticed! Surely that is the greater miracle?

5. The disciples were hallucinating.

This is another popular reductionist explanation for the Easter Faith of the disciples and the field of psychology is often induced to strengthen it. Jack Kent's 1999 book The Psychological Origins of the Resurrection Myth uses some anecdotal evidence of modern hallucinatory experiences following bereavement and extrapolates a hypothesis that the disciples, overcome with grief, hallucinated and essentially dreamed up the post-Resurrection experiences. Mary Magdalene, the Emmaus road experience and the appearance to the five hundred would also have to fall into this category.

Certainly it is documented that people do have hallucinations following a bereavement. Kent reports that, according to a survey, 47% of widowed spouses have grief-related hallucinations. However, the question arises, do several hundred people, unrelated, over a period of 40 days, in the wake of a missing body, claim different appearances of the same person? This seems somewhat unique in the history of human psychology.

Rudolf Bultmann and other liberal modernist theologians, may have taken this view and defended the Resurrection by suggesting that it was a true event in the life of the disciples but not Jesus. For Bultmann, the important thing is the "formation of the Easter Faith". However, Barth is quick to point out that there must have been an event to kick-start their faith:

> If [the Easter story] is restricted to the development of the faith of the disciples, what can this mean? A kind of parthenogenesis of faith without any external cause; without any cause in an

external event which begets it? a faith which is in the true and proper sense other-worldly? ... A faith which of itself-without any given reasons can explain the figure of the Crucified and recognise in the Crucified the living Lord? (Barth, CD IV.I section 59, p339)

The fact that the gospel writers are careful to report that the disciples' first reaction to Jesus' appearance was that He was a ghost is important. Not only does it tell us that, in the 1st C, ghostly apparitions were in keeping with Judaism, it also differentiates between a belief in an appearance of a returned man from the dead, and the belief in a real, tangibly resurrected man.

6. There are too many inconsistencies with the texts.

Although there are some seeming inconsistencies - such as the timing and which women were present - the "main ingredients" are all there. Moreover, it adds to the verisimilitude of the narratives that there is this difference: the whole Easter story is an avalanche, an unexpected chaos which results in some order. Emotions are heightened; memories are not completely reliable. Read any four newspaper accounts of the same event and they will all differ slightly. In fact it is only in reading several accounts that the truth can be grasped.

Of course, this links to the next criticism.

7. They're all from the same source.

Although all these accounts of the resurrection come from the Bible, it is erroneous to treat them all as being from the same "source". The Bible did not exist in its current canonical form until several centuries after. Although most New Testament scholars agree that Matthew and Luke draw heavily on Mark, there is also the mysterious, anonymous and hypothetical "Q" (from the Latin Quella, meaning "source") that accounts for common material between Matthew and Luke. The fourth gospel purports to be an eye-witness account (or, to take the liberal view, written by a Johannine community following this tradition). Luke talks about sifting through various traditions and accounts. The letters in the back of a modern New Testament have different authors. Just because they have been collated as a canon of scripture does not make them the same source. Remember that "Bible" really means "library". As such, the warrant of multiple attestation seems to hold a little more weight.

Further, it is precisely this confusion that lends support to the argument that the accounts are genuine. If one were hoping to invent a world religion at the time, one would not select women as the first witnesses to such an important event. Women's testimony was not admissible in court (it was a backward age). Two male witnesses had to agree upon something for it to be accepted as evidence. If the gospel writers were making it all up, they might have done better to have two (or more) male witnesses to the actual resurrection instead of this garbled tale about an empty tomb.

8. There is no eye-witness account of the resurrection itself.

The Virgin birth has been narrated (if not by all gospels), along with scores of other miracles, but not the Resurrection. As Barth comments, "there is a full account of how Jesus suffered and was crucified ad died, but there is no real account of His resurrection. It is simply indicated by a reference to the sign of the empty tomb. Then it is quietly presupposed in the form of attestations of appearances of the Resurrected. This is all the more striking because the Gospels did fully narrate and describe other resurrections, that of Jairus' daughter (Mt. 9:18-25), that of the young man at Nain (Luke 7:11-16), and that of Lazarus (John 11)." (CD, p334) Perhaps it is not narrated because no one saw it. Barth's conclusion is that "here it is not possible to speak of someone superior to Jesus Christ who took Him by the hand and by his word called Him to life from the dead. Here we can think only of the act of God which cannot be described and therefore cannot be narrated, and then of the actual fact that Jesus Himself stood in the midst."

It is, however, narrated in the apocryphal "Gospel of Peter". This was recovered in 1886 and is generally dated around the mid-2nd C. Although, in the text, it claims to be written by Peter, it is almost certainly not. It does, however, contain some rather surprising supernatural elements:

> *[9] And in the night in which the Lord's day was drawing on, as the soldiers kept guard two by two in a watch, there was a great voice in the heaven; and they saw the heavens opened, and two men descend with a great light and approach the tomb. And the stone that was put at the door rolled of itself and made way in part; and the tomb was opened, and both the young men entered in. [10] When therefore those soldiers saw it, they awakened the centurion and the elders, for they too were close by keeping guard. And as they declared what things they had seen, again they saw three men come forth from the tomb, and two of them supporting one, and a cross following them. And the heads of the two reached to heaven, but the head of him who was led by them overpassed the heavens. And they heard a voice from the heavens, saying, "You have preached to them that sleep." And a response was heard from the cross, "Yes."*

Not only does the cross itself float and speak (!), but the ascension seems to occur directly after the resurrection. Even if this had been dated at the same time as the other gospels, it does not seem to fit with the rest of the evidence and is thus discounted.

This leaves us with the main problem for believing the "miracle" of the Resurrection.

9. There is a paucity of empirical evidence.

David Hume declares that "A wise man ... proportions his belief to the evidence" and the problem is that there really does seem to be no empirical evidence for it. Then again, neither is there empirical evidence to falsify it.

The story of "doubting Thomas" related in John 20:24-29 could be seen in a slightly different light. Thomas has been somewhat vilified for refusing to accept his friends' testimony that Jesus has risen but his scepticism surely places him as among the wise, according to Hume. It is worth noting that, although Hume offers in in depth critique of miracles, his position is one of intellectual scepticism. He does not categorically deny miracles but instead insists that, "no testimony is sufficient to establish a miracle, unless the testimony be of such a kind, that its falsehood would be more miraculous, than the fact, which it endeavors to establish". Although he does not talk directly about the Resurrection of Jesus in his famous passage on Miracles, Hume does say this:

> When anyone tells me, that he saw a dead man restored to life, I immediately consider with myself, whether it be more probable, that this person should either deceive or be deceived, or that the fact, which he relates, should really have happened. I weigh the one miracle against the other; and according to the superiority,

which I discover, I pronounce my decision, and always reject the greater miracle. If the falsehood of his testimony would be more miraculous, than the event which he relates; then, and not till then, can he pretend to command my belief or opinion.

Proponents of the Resurrection will say that the "greater miracle" is the reductionist explanation. Sceptics will hold the opposing view. "Doubting Thomas" is simply an empiricist. When presented with (what he considers to be) empirical evidence for the Resurrection, he not only accepts the miracle, but makes the theological and Christological leap, in faith, to declare Jesus "my Lord and my God".

This is all well and good but, 2,000 years later, is there any empirical evidence for us to examine?

The Turin Shroud is, perhaps, the most notorious claimant of empirical evidence in support of the Resurrection.

Far too many books, articles and documentaries have been produced on the subject to fully disseminate here but a brief overview is given:

The shroud - a linen cloth - bears the image of a man who appears to have suffered some sort of bodily trauma in keeping with crucifixion. The image appears much more clearly in negative colours, under X-ray, than in its original sepia. This negative image was first observed in 1898. As of 2014, there is still no consensus as to the dating of the shroud. Some late-20th C carbon dating would have it a medieval forgery; however, it has been shown that the fragment of the cloth dated seemed to belong to a more recent addition to the cloth - some sort of repair work.

A further mystery is how the image was transferred on to the cloth. It is only found on the first few layers of the cloth and current scholarship has yet to demonstrate how it could be reproduced. According to a report in the Independent newspaper, "a short and intense burst of UV directional radiation can colour a linen cloth so as to reproduce many of the peculiar characteristics of the body image on the Shroud of Turin ... [but] this degree of power cannot be reproduced by any normal UV source built to date." Believers conclude that the power of the Resurrection imprinted the image.

Anatomically correct, the image almost certainly depicts a man with wounds to the head, shoulders, wrists, feet and back which corroborate the Passion narratives in the gospels. This strongly suggests that it was wrapped around the body of a man who underwent the traumas as recorded in the gospels. Whether this was Jesus or some poor unfortunate medieval fellow who was tortured in such a way to create the hoax is impossible to verify. Even if it is Jesus' burial cloth, it is not necessarily empirical evidence for the Resurrection, only the crucifixion and burial, but if there is a natural explanation for the image on the shroud, it has yet to be explained.

SCIENCE AND MIRACLES

Miracles is one area which seems to unite Science and Religion more than divide it, as religious communities turn to Science to verify their supernatural claims and Science comes up short at providing explanations for every miracle story.

However, as we see in the case of the continuing mystery of the Turin Shroud, "Science" cannot rely upon empiricism alone but needs to engage with historical and theological criticism.

Returning to Hume's advice to weigh up the evidence and come down on the side of whichever is the "lesser" miracle, some will continue to believe it a greater miracle that a man could walk on water, while others believe that a man trained dolphins to make it appear that he did. Still others, such as Morton Smith, take to "explaining" the miracles of Jesus as illusionary tricks and, drawing parallels with other "magicians" of the era, simply reduce the gospel accounts to re-workings of other miraculous stories:

> *Moses divided the sea and walked through (Ex. 14.2 IfF.), Jesus simply walked over it (Mk. 6.48f.p.; Jn. 6.19) - another brilliant piece of one-upmanship, but not likely to have occurred to the evangelists had there not been a story of Jesus' walking on the water, as magicians were expected to. (Morton Smith, Jesus The Magician, 1978)*

This argument is taken up by Dawkins, who reports that:

> *Robert Gillooly shows how all the essential features of the Jesus legend, including the star in the east, the virgin birth, the veneration of the baby by kings, the miracles, the execution, the*

resurrection and the ascension are borrowed - every last one of them - from other religions already in existence in the Mediterranean and Near East region.

However, just because there are similarities does not mean that they did not really happen, once, in Palestine (nor does it mean they did) - the similarity of miracle stories from different cultures once convinced the atheistic CS Lewis they were all made up, but he later came to believe that "the story of Christ is simply a true myth: a myth working on us in the same way as he others, but with this tremendous difference that it really happened." Moreover, even if Smith's thesis is correct in his supposition that the gospel writers are simply playing "one-upmanship" with Moses, it does not solve the problem of the prior claim of a miracle performed by Moses.

However liberal a view one tries to take, we cannot simply de-mythologise every religion. As Dawkins observes, "the miracle-free religion defended by Gould would not be recognised by most practising theists in the pew or on the prayer mat".

This is why the role of Science is so crucial in today's religions - if miracles are to be believed, they must be demonstrated **NOT TO BE FALSIFIED** by empiricism:

Did Jesus have a human father, or was his mother a virgin at the time of his birth? Whether or not there is enough surviving evidence to decide it, this is still a strictly scientific question with a definite answer in principle: yes or no. Did Jesus raise Lazarus from the dead? Did he himself come alive again, three days after being crucified? There is an answer to every such question, whether or not we can discover it in practice, and it is a strictly scientific answer. The methods we should use to settle the matter, in the unlikely event that relevant evidence ever became available, would be purely and entirely scientific methods. To dramatize the point, imagine, by some remarkable set of circumstances, that forensic archaeologists unearthed DNA evidence to show that Jesus really did lack a biological father. Can you imagine religious apologists shrugging their shoulders and saying anything remotely like the following? "Who cares? Scientific evidence is completely irrelevant to theological questions. Wrong magisterium! We're concerned only with ultimate questions and with moral values. Neither DNA nor any other scientific evidence could ever have any bearing on the matter, one way or the other." (Dawkins, The God Delusion)

While the jury is still out on some miracles, the religious believer and the sceptic find themselves aboard Mitchell's ship, approaching land or not, having to make a decision based upon the balance of probability and the accumulation of evidence.

KEY TERMS

- **CESSATIONISM** - The position that God has stopped performing miracles.

- **CHRISTOLOGY** - A branch of theology concerned with the personhood of Jesus of Nazareth, ie his divinity/humanity.

- **CREDO QUIA ABSURDUM EST** - "I believe because it is absurd." (Tertullian)

- **DOCTRINE** - Church teaching.

- **DUNAMIS** - "Deeds of power" - the word used by Mark, Matthew and Luke to refer to Jesus' miracles.

- **EX NIHILO** - Out of nothing.

- **FAVOURITISM/PARTIALITY** - A complaint that miracles show God has "favourites" as He does not heal everybody.

- **IF GOD, THEN GOD ...** - The hypothesis that if God exists, then He would be capable of certain actions.

- **INCARNATION** - The Christian doctrine that God became man in the person of Jesus of Nazareth.

- **LAWS OF NATURE** - Truths about the universe currently held by science, eg gravity.

- **MIRACLE** - "A transgression of a law of nature by a particular volition of the Deity, or by the interposition of some invisible agent." (Hume)

- **MULTIPLE ATTESTATION** - If several different sources say the same, or similar things, it is more credible and, perhaps, likely to be true.

- **RESURRECTION** - One of the tenets of the Christian faith - the belief that Jesus was raised to new life on the Sunday after his crucifixion.

- **SEMION** - "Sign" - the word used by John to refer to Jesus' miracles.

- **SPACETIME** - The observation that matter has duration and that time and space are inextricably linked.

- **SUPRA** - Beyond.

- **TETRAGRAMMATON** - Literally "four letters" - representing the Name of God revealed to Moses, in Exodus 3:14 widely transliterated as YHWH or Yahweh.

- **THEODICY** - Justification of God in the face of suffering.

- **TURIN SHROUD** - Mysterious cloth believed, by some, to be the burial shroud of Jesus. It bears an image of what appears to be a crucified man.

SELF-ASSESSMENT QUESTIONS

1. What is the role of faith in understanding miracles?

2. Explain what is meant by "the laws of nature" and why it is important for discussions about miracles.

3. Can the philosophical problems of miracles be solved a priori?

4. Can God perform miracles?

5. "The empiricist must falsify every miracle story to declare that miracles are impossible." To what extent do you agree?

6. Write an article for a 1st C newspaper in support of, or against, the Resurrection of Jesus.

7. Watch some documentaries on the Turin Shroud and conduct further research. Hoax or genuine - which is the "greater miracle"?

8. How far would you agree that miracles from different religious traditions pose a problem for faith?

9. How important is the role of Science in the field of miracles?

10. Research modern miracle stories.

Quantum Physics

"Quantum Mechanics is weird. That's just the way it is." (Seth Lloyd, MIT)

If "seeing is believing", then Quantum Physics is about to change everything:

What we have, hitherto, been talking about is empiricism - the notion that reality is understood, according to the scientific method, from observation and measurement. In Quantum Mechanics, observation actually constructs the reality. This sort of topsy-turvy approach to Science is not only confusing to laymen but to scientists, especially theoretical physicists and those actually "doing" the quantum mechanics.

Without a few post-doctoral degrees in the field it is difficult to do the subject justice, and there is simply not enough room in this Study Guide to expound beyond some rudimentary summaries of the important theses and how they relate to the general philosophical study of Science and Religion. For non-specialists, a good starting point will be YouTube - where you can trawl through scores of documentaries on the subject. Here, though, the general principle of observation and superposition of states is outlined.

QUANTUM LEAP

Sadly, nothing to do with Scott Bakula's adventures in the much-beloved television series, the Quantum Leap was first proposed by Danish physicist **NEILS BOHR** (1885-1962), following an observation that certain heated gases, when looked at through a prism, make distinct lines of light visible.

Bohr theorised that electrons could only move around an atom in fixed orbits but that, when heated, electrons make a **QUANTUM LEAP** to another fixed orbit, giving off visible light. However, it does this without going in the space in between; it simply "jumps" from one orbit to another.

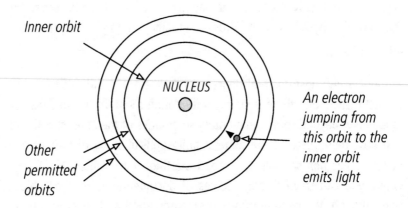

Inner orbit

NUCLEUS

Other permitted orbits

An electron jumping from this orbit to the inner orbit emits light

The Bohr model of an atom

Bohr argued that electrons' energy comes in discrete, minute chunks which he called quanta. Thus, the quantum is concerned with the smallest level of reality and the minimum amount of any physical entity.

BOHR VERSUS EINSTEIN

Traditional Psychics holds that the universe is predictable - essentially an ordered cosmos. As we have seen in our discussion of Miracles, this is axiomatic for any discussion of divine intervention. However, Bohr's wider implications seem to blow this thesis out of the water.

Double-slit experiment

Marbles are fired at a wall which has two equal holes in it. Behind the wall is a cloth or material that records a mark, once hit by the marbles. Every time a particular area of the material is hit, the mark recorded is darker. After the experiment, the material behind the wall is examined.

It seems that although (as we might expect), the material behind the wall is darker at the areas directly behind the holes, there are also dark spots elsewhere; moreover, there are places on the material that have never been hit by the marble. (This, according to general consensus, is true for the results of every similar experiment.)

The pattern on the material conforms more to the pattern of waves than it does to particles. Waves interact with each other - sometimes strengthening each other, sometimes cancelling each other out. Waves can split and combine. It is this that creates the striped pattern and means, as **EUGENE KUTORYANSKY** explains, that "all objects behave like waves". However, for a wave to produce this striped pattern on the material behind the wall, the waves would have to pass through both the holes SIMULTANEOUSLY, and only one marble is shot through at a time.

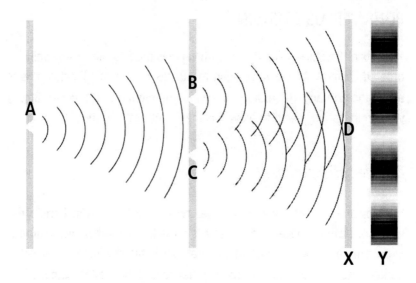

The image shows how the particle, if acting as a wave, would simultaneously pass through both slits (B and C) and create a series of waves combining and splitting with each other that results in the wave hitting the back of the screen (X) at the point (D), creating the pattern (Y). If the particle were to remain acting as a particle, it could only pass through one of the splits - (B) or (C).

At the subatomic level (and it should be noted that this experiment uniquely works with small things), this firing of particles through a double slit is more acutely observed. However, the notion that a particle behaves as a wave presents a paradox - how can an electron be both a particle and a wave?

Then again, how can Jesus be fully God and fully man for Christians? Indeed, the paradoxical nature of this field of science might be used by the faithful to add weight to theological claims - almost as if nature itself has the quintessential paradox of the God-man stamped on its subatomic heart.

Max Born (1882-1970) suggested that the wave produced by the double-slit experiment was a probability wave. Looking at the size of the wave at any location in its journey will indicate its probability of hitting any one spot at the other side of the wall. The electron itself is simply a jumble of possibilities. This is because, according to Bohr, before you measure or observe a particle, its characteristics are uncertain.

This is what makes Quantum Physics so different from Classical Physics - the suggestion that when you measure a particle, it forces the particle to make a choice as to where it will end up. Einstein particularly disagreed with this view, as shall be explored below. As a side note, this may remind the Sociology student of the **HAWTHORNE EFFECT** - the notion that human participants in an experiment subconsciously alter their behaviour if they know they are being observed. (Of course this parallel somewhat anthropomorphises electrons.)

Quantum spin and entanglement

According to Quantum Mechanics, electrons "spin". However, this spin is erratic, or "fuzzy" - they spin neither "clockwise" nor "anticlockwise" (quotation marks are used because the way in which electrons are said to spin is analogous to the spinning of a sphere or, say, the Earth) until observed.

Quantum physicists suggest that, sometimes, particles can become entangled, ie inextricably and irrevocably linked. Usually this is happens when particles come into close proximity with each other. However, once separated - even if they were to be put at different ends of the universe -

the two particles **REMAIN ENTANGLED**. The fun really starts to happen when ONE of the electrons is measured; it is always found that the **OTHER** electron in the entangled pair spins in the opposite direction. For example, Particle 1 is measured and observed spinning in direction A. Particle 2 will always spin in direction B. This happens even when the two entangled particles are separated by extraordinary distances.

Einstein, however, was unconvinced that the act of observation or measuring affected the particle, and said:

> I think that a particle must have a separate reality independent of the measurements. That is: an electron has spin, location and so forth even when it is not being measured. I like to think that the moon is there even if I am not looking at it.

An analogy of a pair of gloves is used by physicist Brian Greene: Suppose that your friend takes a pair of gloves and puts one of the gloves in a box and the other in a separate box. She posts one box to you and the second to a mutual friend in Australia. When you receive your box, you do not know whether or not yours contains the left, or the right, hand glove - up until you open the box, there is equal probability of it being either. However, as soon as you open the box and see it is (say) the right-hand glove, you know that your friend in Australia must have the left-hand glove (assuming the postal system is as (in)efficient on that side of the world as here!) Your act of opening the box and looking has not decided the outcome of which glove was in which box. The right-hand glove was always in your box and the left hand glove, always in the box in Australia.

In the same way, argued Einstein, particles' spin is determined before you look.

Bohr disagreed, but seeing as the only way to solve this required measuring the particles, and since this (according to Bohr's idea) would affect the spin of the particles, the debate seemed to be at an impasse.

However, in 1967, a postgraduate student at Columbia University, **JOHN CLAUSER**, used Irish physicist John Bell's paper to build a machine that could settle the debate. The maths is particularly complicated and can be investigated independently, but suffice it to say that the scientific community have largely accepted that Einstein was wrong and that, had he lived long enough to see the experiment and its results, Einstein would have happily admitted his erroneous position.

Of course, if the problem can only be solved with experimentation, the question arises whether a) the experiment will have had some causal effect on the outcome, if we apply the hypothesis of observation b) whether Classical Physics and Quantum Physics are really so different? When the chips are down, it seems empiricism will always win out.

Schrödinger's Cat

This is a fairly infamous thought experiment, popularised recently by a reference to it in American sitcom The Big Bang Theory. Erwin Schrödinger was an Austrian quantum physicist who used the idea of a cat placed in a box to highlight the absurdity of the Copenhagen interpretation of superposition of states (the notion that a particle can be simultaneously two things at once).

Imagine a cat is placed in a box with a radioactive substance, a Geiger counter and some cyanide. The box is sealed (let us assume with some holes for the cat to breathe through). If, at any time, the Geiger counter detects that one of the radioactive particles has decayed, then the bottle of cyanide is smashed and the cat killed.

The Copenhagen interpretation holds that particles simultaneously exist in all states at once, until observed, but it would be absurd to think that, until observed, the cat is both dead and alive.

Some quantum physicists suggest that there are an infinite number of parallel universes for every possible outcome. When the box is opened, two realities are created: one in which the cat is alive, and one in which it is dead.

We could update this thought experiment to the example of the television game show Deal Or No Deal, in which the game contestant is given a sealed box with one of 22 possible money amounts in, ranging from 1p to £250,000. The other 21 boxes are held by other game participants. The contestant chooses five boxes to open in the first round. As half the boxes contain amounts under £1,000, the contestant will hope to reveal lower amounts. The Bank then makes an offer to the contestant - either he can "deal" for the amount offered, or continue to play, hoping that his box contains a higher monetary figure than he is offered.

Eventually, (provided there is "no deal") only two boxes remain - the contestant's box and one other. If the Copenhagen interpretation is correct, then the act of looking in the box will determine the amount of money in it.

Again, we see why this is a ridiculous position for the contestant to hold: no one in their right minds would play the game if they thought that the amounts in the box were subject to a state of permanent flux. Although it does mean, according to the parallel worlds model, that there is a world in which every Deal Or No Deal contestant has gone away with £250,000.

IMPLICATIONS FOR PHILOSOPHY OF RELIGION

Causation

At base, the universe is described by inherent probabilistic theory and that is highly counter-intuitive and something many people would find difficulty accepting. (Edward Farhi, MIT)

Quantum mechanics seems to challenge notions such as cause and effect. If particles can simultaneously be in two states, can flicker in and out of existence, does this mean that the universe might simply flicker in and out of existence as in the oscillating model? This seems to put a spanner in the works for proponents of cosmological arguments for the existence of God.

However, the difficulty for quantum physics is applying it to the everyday world. Why can things at the quantum level remain so uncertain when we are either here or not? What happens on the quantum (subatomic) level does not seem to be true of the macro world - the universe we engage and participate in. Although proponents of quantum physics may simply assert that it does, it seems analogous to the "God of the gaps" objection.

Quantum Physics is largely about probabilities and it is noted by its champions that these predictions are verified through experimentation again and again. Including Quantum Mechanics in calculations has led to advances in electronics and computing. By a similar token, religious believers might say that incorporating God into a worldview provides a complete explanation of the cosmos. This is very reminiscent of Leibniz's principle of **SUFFICIENT REASON**: for the quantum physicist, her view provides sufficient reason to explain the universe. For the theist, God completes the picture. Perhaps scientists and theologians are not so very different?

Analogy

The very act of going from the quantum to the macro - of using cats and gloves to explain what is happening to electrons - smacks of religious parables and analogies. Descartes' observation in his third Meditation that "it is of the nature of the infinite that it should not be comprehended by the finite" seems applicable here, by analogy.

Indeed, it is this correlation between Quantum Physics and Religion that provides a new analogy which encapsulates and explicates the so-called "problems" of religious language.

Just as Aquinas properly observed that we cannot use language univocally to talk about God (for to say "God loves you" in the same way that "I love my brother" is ridiculous), neither can we say that the electron spins on axes in the same way that the Earth rotates. Neither can language be applied to God equivocally (ie in a completely different way; for to say that God's love is nothing like the love I have for my brother is unsatisfactory). If the "spinning" of the electron and the "earth" were mere equivocations, then the word would be useless, as it would form no picture in the mind. Rather, then, both the spinning of the electron and the love of God must be understood (and are being used) analogously.

Wittgenstein's theory of language games is also helpful in drawing a parallel between the way in which scientific and religious language work. Having to be "in the game", we realise, once more, that all language is about use. Thus it is no stranger for the quantum physicist to claim "the cat in the box exists in a superposition of states of being dead and alive", than the declaration of faith that "Jesus is both fully man and fully God".

Predestination

The gloves, cat and Deal Or No Deal box invoke and evoke debates about predestination. If our act of observation alters the reality, to what extent is matter "free"? Schrödinger's Cat is particularly useful in making the philosophical point that, even if God knows the outcome of our choices, it does not mean that we do not make them freely. Of course, the Copenhagen interpretation would seem to support predestination - if God, in His omniscience, "sees" or observes humanity, then the act of His observing would, presumably determine our actions.

This might not be very satisfactory to advocates of free will, and many prefer CS Lewis' idea that God perceives all times as present because of His being supranatural (ie, beyond nature). Thus, although He "knows" what choices we will make because He sees us making them at the time, His observation does not impede our freedom.

Anthropic Principle

If reality is indeed shaped by our observation, it has interesting implications for the Anthropic Principle as related in the section above on design arguments. If the moon only exists in the way that it does because we look at it, some might argue that this is suggestive of a world purposefully designed for humans.

The (somewhat tired) riddle "If a tree falls in a forest and there's no one to hear it, does it fall?" might be invoked here. Of course, one of the conundrums is whether or not it needs to be a human observer. Moreover, this presents real difficulties with evolution and the existence and formation of the universe before life, as well as those areas of the universe as yet unobserved. Presumably this is because, quantum physicists would rightly point out, the philosopher has catastrophically failed to really comprehend Quantum Mechanics and has simply reduced it to a ludicrous "pop theory" that no physicist actually believes. By the same token, the believer might reply that this is simply what the atheist does to God - set up a straw god or man-in-the-sky no serious theologian believes in and says "boo!" to it.

Uncertainty

> Don't ask me why, or how it works - that is an illegal question. All we can say is, that is apparently the way the world ticks. (Walter Lewin, MIT)

Towards the end of the seventh season of The Big Bang Theory, Dr Sheldon Cooper - a promising theoretical physicist, infamous for his disparaging remarks about experimental Physics and other scientific disciplines - has an epiphany that results in a form of apostasy.

> LEONARD: You've been working on String Theory for the last 20 years, and you're no closer to proving it than when you started.

> SHELDON: Yeah, well, I've had a lot on my plate! ... Am I wasting my life on a theory that can never be proven?

> [... Later to Penny:]

I've devoted my life to string theory and its quest for the compactification of extra dimensions. I've got nothing to show for it, and I feel like a fool.

The uncertainty that Quantum Physics is enshrouded in is part of its appeal and part of what makes it so difficult for laymen to understand or even take seriously. If quantum physicists themselves cannot seem to make their minds up about string theory or dark matter, then how can we be expected to trust any science? Surely it's all guesswork? The danger here, of course, is to "throw out the baby with the bathwater". Should we ditch our laws of gravity because electrons may or may not be affected by our observation? Do problems in understanding black holes invalidate evolutionary biology?

Some might reply in the affirmative and suggest that science is trying to pull the proverbial wool over our eyes by claiming to describe reality and truth, when really it is all guesswork and mystery. This hardly seems fair, although a more moderate approach might be to realise that Science is not "an exact science", and scientific truth hardly "gospel".

The uncertainty of Quantum Physics also strengthens the case for the compatibility (even similarity) between Science and Religion: the Mysterious is an important aspect of theology and philosophy.

"Which of us comprehendeth the Almighty Trinity?" asks St Augustine. The otherness of God is an essential component of any theological system, and one Karl Barth is keen to defend. When asked by a student what the greatest theological insight of his career was, Barth (having written some six million words of theology) replied: "Jesus loves me, this I know, for the Bible tells me so." It might not be explicable or defendable philosophically, but if God is God then there must be a certain ineffability and a certain mystery that remains hidden.

Stephen Hawking famously closes his book A Brief History Of Time with the following observation:

> However, if we discover a complete theory, it should in time be understandable by everyone, not just by a few scientists. Then we shall all, philosophers, scientists and just ordinary people, be able to take part in the discussion of the question of why it is that we and the universe exist. If we find the answer to that, it would be the ultimate triumph of human reason - for then we should know the mind of God.

Dawkins is quick to assure his readers that Hawking was only using the word "God" metaphorically, but it seems the only true difference between the quantum physicist trying to explain and understand the universe with a complete theory, and the theologian, is that Hawking supposes we can ascend out of the cave (to use Plato's analogy). The religious believer thinks we must be pulled out - we can understand only when God reaches down. The starting point for the scientist is humanity; for the theologian, revelation. The philosopher is possibly between the two positions, depending on the degree of his agnosticism.

However, it is this uncertainty that gives way to hope for scientist, philosopher and theologian: "Now we see but through a glass darkly; then, face to face: now I know in part; but then I shall know even as also I am known." (1 Corinthians 13:12)

KEY TERMS

- **ANALOGICAL** - Using the same word in a similar way.

- **COPENHAGEN INTERPRETATION** - In Quantum Mechanics, this is the view that quantum theory does not describe reality but that observation forms reality.

- **COSMOS** - A view of the universe as an ordered entity.

- **EQUIVOCAL** - Using the same word in a completely different way.

- **PARADOX** - Two conflicting ideas held together. A contradiction in terms.

- **QUANTUM ENTANGLEMENT** - A physical phenomenon that occurs when pairs or groups of particles come to be inextricably linked together.

- **QUANTUM PHYSICS** - Branch of physics dealing with "reality" at the nano, or subatomic, level.

- **QUANTUM LEAP** - Bohr's theory that electrons "leap" from orbit to orbit around a nucleus when heat is applied.

- **STRING THEORY** - A branch of theoretical physics that is a candidate for a "theory of everything".

- **SUFFICIENT REASON** - Leibniz' view that all events must ultimately be explicable in terms of the reasons a divine being would have had for choosing one alternative rather than another.

- **SUPERPOSITION OF STATES** - A particle is supposed to be simultaneously in more than one state.

- **SUPRANATURAL** - Beyond nature (as opposed to "supernatural" - above nature).

- **UNIVOCAL** - Using the same word in the same way.

SELF-ASSESSMENT QUESTIONS

1. How does Quantum Physics differ from "Classical Physics"?

2. Write an article summarising the Bohr-Einstein debate.

3. Further research and perform your own double-slit experiment.

4. "As it is impossible to falsify the claim that electrons are in an erratic state of quantum spin before observing it, Quantum Physics amounts to a faith claim." Assess this view.

5. Explain how Schrödinger's Cat challenges the Copenhagen interpretation of Quantum Physics.

6. "Quantum Physics disproves the cosmological argument for the existence of God." How far do you agree?

7. "Quantum Physics presents as many challenges to classical science as it does to religion." How far do you agree?

8. "Quantum Physics highlights the unknowability of the universe and, as such, turns Science into a belief system indistinguishable from religion." What do you think?

9. "Quantum Physics proposes a universe in which miracles are philosophically impossible." Assess this view.

10. What does Quantum Physics ultimately add to the debate between Science and Religion?

Science AND Religion

"WHAT IS TRUTH?"

This quintessential question, attributed to Pilate in John's gospel, is what the debates between Science and Religion come down to. It is the attempt to resolve the epistemological trauma of our unknowing; the desire to apprehend the currently incomprehensible. It cannot be that Science and Religion are not so diametrically opposed that they do not, in their own ways, attempt to answer this question.

The anti-realist simply subjectifies truth and says, "The Virgin Birth is true within Christianity but not Judaism." This essentially says nothing. The realist who believes there is an objective truth (even if currently unknown) says, "The Virgin Birth is either true or false and we hope to know the answer one day." Both Science and Religion must essentially adopt the realist approach, or there could be no disagreements. However, perhaps a more pertinent question is: "Where is truth?"

> Science studies nature. And the question is whether anything besides nature exists - anything "outside". How could you find that out by studying nature? (CS Lewis, "Religion and Science", 1945)

Science looks within the universe because only the universe is empirically observable. Religion posits what is outside of the universe but only has the tools within the universe to dispose its work. One might conclude that it will, therefore, ultimately fail, even if its hypotheses are correct. Aquinas's "Ways" posit the existence of a Prime Mover for the universe from observation of the universe, and this methodology has been criticised as an intrinsic weakness of his argument.

However, the recent discovery of gravitational waves seem to support the (scientific) hypothesis of a finite universe, and it is not impossible (or even implausible) to suggest that something other than the universe had to "start it off".

Really, both Philosophy and Science must concede the limits of knowledge on the empirical front. We will turn our attention to the fundamental nature of the relationship between Science and Religion, by considering the four models which Professor Dennis Alexander of St Edmund's College, Cambridge proposes.

THE CONFLICT MODEL

Science and religion are in irresolvable conflict ... there is no way in which you can be both properly scientifically minded and a true religious believer. James Worrell

This would seem to be the view held by Richard Dawkins, who regales the "cautionary tale" of Kurt Wise, a "promising" and well-educated geologist who saw his belief in the Young Earth model of creation as conflicting with his knowledge of Geology. Taking a pair of scissors, he cut out every verse he deemed incompatible with a scientific worldview until there was so little left that he realised he would have to make a choice between Science and Religion. He chose the former and writes that he, "in great sorrow, tossed into the fire all my dreams and hopes in science".

Dawkins rightly points out that all Wise "had to do was toss out the Bible. Or interpret it symbolically, or allegorically, as the theologians do." Of course, the subtext here is that Dawkins is suggesting that theologians move goalposts so as to not to have to engage with the difficulties of maintaining faith in the face of empirical evidence. However, although some believers might do this, as this book's chapter on Origins has highlighted, there are several different interpretations of scripture which precede evolutionary theory. One might argue that Ward simply misunderstood his Bible: his Harvard education was in Science, not Theology, after all. Indeed, former Archbishop Rowan Willams asks:

Is [Creationism] reading the Bible correctly? Is it understanding what kind of text the Bible is? I think the first couple of chapters of Genesis tell us what we need to know: what is, exists because God invites it into being.

One can be a scientist and not believe every scientific claim or theory, just as one can be religious and not accept every miracle story or religious doctrine. Indeed, religious believers are highly selective: to be a Christian means to reject the Hindu belief in reincarnation; to be a Muslim is to herald Jesus as a prophet but not God Incarnate. By the same token, as we have seen, to accept the Copenhagen interpretation of Quantum Physics is to reject Einstein's view. Both the scientist and religious believer select their creeds, or worldviews, in proportion to the evidence they are presented with, and their interpretations of such evidence. In this respect, there is not all that much conflict.

The fact that there really are several scientists who have religious convictions seems to counter the conflict model. Dr Robert Asher says: "Religious scientists are actually quite common."

Google "religious scientists" and you will be able to trawl through thousands of pages written by and about scientists who profess religious faiths. Moreover, it should always be remembered that theology was once heralded the "Queen of Sciences" and that the first scientists were really theologians trying to better understand the Creator through a study of creation (nature).

Of course there will always be areas - specific questions - which Science and Religion seem to come into conflict over. Dawkins, however, cannot have it both ways with his claim that the "God hypothesis" is a "scientific question". As a realist, he writes in The God Delusion:

> *Either [God] exists or he doesn't. It is a scientific question; one day we may know the answer, and meanwhile we can say something pretty strong about the probability.*

Science cannot pronounce that God does not exist precisely (as per Lewis' observation above) because it is concerned with the natural, empirical world (or universe) and Religion is talking about the supernatural. In the words of Asher:

> One comprehension of a natural mechanism is independent of a potential agency behind it; we can no more assert atheism due to our understanding of evolution than claim the non-existence of Thomas Edison due to our understanding of electricity.

THE NOMA MODEL

This has largely been addressed in the first chapter of this Study Guide, but is worth revisiting briefly:

Gould's idea of Non-Overlapping Magisteria seems almost a diplomatic answer to the question: suggesting that Science and Religion are really talking about different things - asking and answering different questions - makes any conflict somewhat redundant. Countries might go to war over a border dispute. No country would go to war if the dispute were over completely different borders. The fact that Science and Religion are engaged in specific debates; that religion seeks empirical evidence before claiming a miracle has occurred and that science cites empirical evidence to falsify religious dogmas demonstrates the absurdity of holding the NOMA position for too long. Scientists, philosophers and theologians are all trying to understand the origins of the universe.

THE FUSION MODEL(S)

This position, described by Alexander as the "polar opposite" of NOMA, holds that Science and Religion are essentially the same thing and that scientific theories are the same as religious ideas, albeit in different language: so that Buddhism is compatible with Quantum Mechanics. This smudges the distinction between the two disciplines and, according to the faith tradition, either supposes that all knowledge belongs to the same reality - be it religious or scientific - as in Eastern traditions, or that knowledge of religion and science are part of revelation. Some creationists, for example, seek to present dogma as science (such as Intelligent Design).

Alexander is careful to note that there are so many different models that each should be assessed individually. However, a general point is that "fusion models go well beyond natural theology in proposing that the actual content of science informs the content of religious belief and vice versa".

However, one of the disadvantages with adopting a fusion model is that it ceases to allow science to be a truly impartial and distinctive discipline. Science might ultimately seek to answer the deeper questions of purpose, but it does not have to in order to be useful. As divorced from religion, science can carry out work independently and, perhaps more importantly, in collaboration with scientists who share different philosophical and religious convictions.

THE COMPLEMENTARY MODEL

This sounds like a bit of a "middle way" - suggesting that Science and Religion look at things from different perspectives and provide explanations that complement each other, rather than being rivals. As Alexander explains:

> *The language of complementarity was originally introduced by the physicist Niels Bohr to describe the relationship between the particle and wave descriptions of matter; it was necessary to hold on to both understandings simultaneously to do justice to the data. Since Bohr's time the idea of complementarity has been greatly extended within the science-religion field to encompass any entity that requires explanations at multiple levels in order to explain its complexity adequately.*

An illustration of how different academic fields complement each other to build up a coherent picture might be drawn with the ways in which a radiographer, oncologist, general practitioner and surgeon might all be involved with understanding a patient's cancer.

The famous parable of the blind men and the elephant is also useful: several blind men touch various parts of an elephant and conclude, according to the area touched, that the beast is like a fan, wall, spear, snake, tree or rope. Of course, only when all parts of knowledge are added together can something resembling the truth be learned.

This is the obvious appeal of the complementary model: it takes both science and religion seriously. The danger is that it slides very easily into the NOMA camp and fails to address the very real differences between the two. Furthermore, there is a risk of representing science as "objective" to the apparent "subjectivity" of religious faith. Alexander points out that this belies the sometimes objective nature of religious claims, such as "moral facts" but it also belies the subjective nature of science, as we saw - in particular - in Quantum Physics.

If none of these models are wholly satisfactory, the question of Science and Religion seems to have no answer. Perhaps this is the case, but there is another category of thinking to propose.

THE IMAGINAL

Are we humans because we look at the stars or do we look at the stars because we're human? (Stardust, 2006)

By the **IMAGINAL** is meant: "with recourse to the imagination but not necessarily 'made up'".

To imagine is to see beyond what is immediately present. All humans do this in everyday life, and Science and Religion are no different.

It is the faculty of the imagination that fills the gaps in what is unknown, invites wonder and sparks curiosity. Invention and discovery start with and are fuelled by imagination, which is surely the precursor to creation - both human and divine: Bohr's imagination led him to think beyond what was known; Darwin's imagination saw a commonality in animal behaviour; St John's imagination let him see Jesus' empty tomb "and believe". (An atheist will, of course, remark that the third example stands apart from the other two in that John imagined something that "did not happen" [ie the Resurrection]. A Creationist will argue that Darwin similarly "invented" evolution. Neither argument is useful. The real point here is to notice the role the imaginal plays in formation of Science and Religion.)

The most obvious application of the imaginal is in narratives. From the cradle, we are used to received truth and ideas as Story. Jesus spoke in parables for a good reason - indeed, the same reason that Dawkins titled his book on common ancestry The Ancestor's Tale. History, in particular (the word for the academic discipline contains the word in the English language) is concerned with stories.

However, it is often the case that Religion and Science are depicted as proffering competing meta-narratives (ie grand stories to explain truths). In this way, both Science and Religion might be considered **MYTHS**. The word "myth" sadly carries negative connotations of falsehood and seems diametrically opposed to historicity, but this is not necessarily so.

Douglas Hedley observes in his book, Living Forms Of The Imagination, that "human beings are amphibious. There is, of course, the being-in-the-world which we experience like any other animal. Yet there is the vast realm of the human imagination which extends far in range temporally and spatially beyond immediate images and after images of proximate objects." As humans, we stand between what we do not know and what we apprehend. Thus we nearly always learn by analogy - drawing on what is known to help us understand what is not. This can only be done with a degree of imagination - almost as if the imaginal is the cement that binds together the bricks of learning in the construction of a storehouse of knowledge and wisdom.

CS Lewis observes that "human intellect is incurably abstract", and explains that "it is only while receiving the myth as a story that you experience the principle concretely ... what flows into you from the myth is not truth but reality (truth is always about something, but reality is about which truth is)." Thus "myth" is not synonymous with "fiction" but, rather, digs at the heart of the matter. Science is as mythic as religion. Hedley says that "the growth of science in various phases of human history, whether in the Athenian or French Enlightenment has the effect of purging much mythical material, but human beings in such intellectually sophisticated and demythologised societies are left with rich mythic and symbolic residue in the cultural environment. We are self-understanding creatures and this symbolic residue pervades human culture." Certainly we have seen already that the modernist theology of the 18th and 19th centuries, as a response to the Enlightenment and advances in Science, sought to "de-mythologise" the Bible. Bultmann was a particular champion of this project; yet it is not only unsatisfactory for the religious believer, it also rests on the false pre-supposition that Science is not mythic or imaginal.

Post-modernism, on the other hand, relativises truth by taking the anti-realist approach. Gustave Flaubert's statement "there is no truth, there is only perception" seems in concordance with Nietzsche's "there are no facts, only interpretations" or Tom Stoppard's "truth is only that which is taken to be true".

All of the above assertions belong to a realist sphere, even if they are anti-realist statements. Just as Ayer's **VERIFICATION PRINCIPLE** fails its own test, any claim that "there is no truth" is tantamount to a truth claim. This is where the post-modern project falls apart. Moreover, it does not seem to remotely describe, explain or satisfy human curiosity and the thirst for truth. Post-modernism is useful, however, in pointing out that all systems of knowledge are essentially meta-narratives, for it is the imaginal that best communicates human knowledge and experience and this is unavoidable. The difference between a strict post-modern, relativistic view of truth and the imaginal understanding of truth is that, to the post-modernist, there can be no objective truth, whereas the imaginal model holds on to a realist understanding of truth that is described and sought after within meta-narratives.

While it is fairly obvious that Religion presents itself as a meta-narrative, it is less obvious that Science also does this. But ask any scientist for an explanation of transfer of energy or cell division and you will be told a narrative. Perhaps it is simply due to our linear existence and, as creatures who subsist in time with a conception of past and future, we turn everything into a history. Moreover, it is the propensity of the academic to "mis-shape the beauteous forms of things" with our "meddling intellect" (Wordsworth).

GK Chesterton makes this apparent in his essay, "Science and Savages":

> The man of science, not realising that ceremonial is essentially a thing which is done without a reason, has to find a reason for every sort of ceremonial, and, as might be supposed, the reason is generally a very absurd one - absurd because it originates not in the simple mind of the barbarian, but in the sophisticated mind of the professor. The learned man will say, for instance,

> The natives of Mumbo-Jumbo Land believe that the dead man can eat and will require food on his journey to the other world. This is attested by the fact that they place food in the grave, and that any family not complying with this rite is the object of the anger of the priests and the tribe.

> To anyone acquainted with humanity, this way of talking is topsy-turvy. It is like saying,

> The English in the twentieth century believed that a dead man could smell. This is attested by the fact that they always covered his grave with lilies, violets, or other flowers. Some priestly and tribal terrors were evidently attached to the neglect of this action, as we have records of several old ladies who were very much disturbed in mind because their wreaths had not arrived in time for the funeral.

The insistence on constructing a narrative is inherent in other fields of Science and forms part of Rowan Williams' criticism of Richard Dawkins.

Williams accuses Dawkins of wrapping everything up in the meta-narrative of a particular version of Darwinian evolution:

> The notion that you can simply extract a highly successful thesis from biology and genetics - evolution, natural selection - and then apply it right across the board to solve every single problem going, I think that really is daft.

Presumably Dawkins might repost something along the lines of "that's exactly what you do - apply the thesis of God and apply it right across the board to solve every single problem!" Which might seem a fair observation were it not for the fact that the "God hypothesis", once accepted, is a genuine candidate for a theory of everything: if God really did create the universe and everything in it, then everything within the universe would ultimately be explained by God. Just as every component of an iPhone can ultimately be explained by Apple - even if the battery or screen might have secondary explanations.

The last part of Sir John Betjeman's much-loved poem "Christmas" makes the point that the greater story, if true, will supersede all others, however equally "true":

> And is it true? And is it true,
> This most tremendous tale of all,
> Seen in a stained-glass window's hue,
> A Baby in an ox's stall?
> The Maker of the stars and sea
> Become a Child on earth for me?
>
> And is it true? For if it is,
> No loving fingers tying strings

Around those tissued fripperies,
The sweet and silly Christmas things,
Bath salts and inexpensive scent
And hideous tie so kindly meant,
No love that in a family dwells,
No carolling in frosty air,
Nor all the steeple-shaking bells
Can with this single Truth compare -

That God was Man in Palestine
And lives to-day in Bread and Wine.

It is precisely this idea of the greater or "better story" that Yann Martel explores in Life Of Pi.

I can well imagine an atheist's last words: "White, white! L-L-Love! My God!" - and the deathbed leap of faith. Whereas the agnostic, if he stays true to his reasonable self, if he stays beholden to dry, yeastless factuality, might try to explain the warm light bathing him by saying, "Possibly a f-f-failing oxygenation of the b-b-brain," and, to the very end, lack imagination and miss the better story.

"WE CANNOT KNOW"

It has been said repeatedly but, once again, it is the epistemological trauma of the human condition that we cannot know. "For I know in part." In this, both Science and Religion are in concordance:

> There can be no complete work, and this is especially the case in the field of theology. (Karl Barth)

> Science is by no means complete ... there's a lot that we don't know - but we're working on it. (Richard Dawkins)

At the end of Martell's Life Of Pi, the eponymous hero converses with two insurance investigators who disbelief his fantastical story:

> "You don't really expect us to believe you, do you? Carnivorous trees? A fish-eating algae that produces fresh water? Tree-dwelling aquatic rodents? These things don't exist."

> "Only because you've never seen them."

> "That's right. We believe what we see."

> "So did Columbus. What do you do when you're in the dark?"

> "Your island is botanically impossible ... Why has no one else come upon it?"

> "It's a big ocean crossed by busy ships. I went slowly, observing much."

"No scientist would believe you."

"These would be the same who dismissed Copernicus and Darwin. Have scientists finished coming upon new plants? In the Amazon basin, for example?"

"Not plants that contradict the laws of nature."

"Which you know through and through?"

"Well enough to know the possible from the impossible."

Mr. Chiba: *"I have an uncle who['s] a bonsai master."*

Pi Patel: *"A what?"*

"A bonsai master. You know, bonsai are little trees."

"You mean shrubs."

"No, I mean trees. Bonsai are little trees ... my uncle has one that is over three hundred years old."

"Three-hundred-year old trees that are two feel tall that you can carry in your arms? ... Whoever heard of such trees? They're botanically impossible."

"But I assure you they exist, Mr. Patel. My uncle -"

"I believe what I see."

Unfortunately Science is often communicated to lay-people as a "complete" paradigm, but this does not reflect the scientific community's own understanding of their project.

Throughout our exploration of Science and Religion, the apparent dichotomies between reason and faith, empiricism and imagination have been at the heart of conflict models. The commonality between the two disciplines is surely in their agnosticism, "believing where we cannot prove". (Tennyson)

However, the gaps in our knowledge do not render the epistemological hopeless. Although "we have but faith: we cannot know; / for knowledge is of things we see", Tennyson continues:

Let knowledge grow from more to more,
But more of reverence in us dwell;
that mind and soul, according well,
May make one music as before.

There will, perhaps, continue to be disagreements between Science and Religion: whether we are alone in the universe; whether we are dependent upon a Creator for our being; whether human consciousness is a function of the brain, or the brain, the manifestation of it. Science may accuse religious believers of inventing a "God of the gaps" as believers call scientific theories "theses of the gaps;" yet, perhaps this is because both Science and Religion are ultimately in agreement with Shakespeare, when he has Hamlet observe: "There are more things in heaven and earth, Horatio, than are dreamt of in your philosophy."

162

KEY TERMS

- **COMPLEMENTARY MODEL** - One of Alexander's four models of the relationship between Science and Religion: a middle way that suggests Science and Religion complement each other, rather than being rivals.

- **CONFLICT MODEL** - One of Alexander's four models of the relationship between Science and Religion: the notion that they are in conflict with each other.

- **FUSION MODEL** - One of Alexander's four models of the relationship between Science and Religion: the opposite of NOMA that suggests Science and Religion can be fused together.

- **IMAGINAL** - Drawing on the imagination, but not necessarily "made up" or "invented". Not to be confused with "imagined".

- **META-NARRATIVE** - A "grand story" that attempts to explain something.

- **MYTH** - An imaginal story. Not necessarily untrue.

- **NARRATIVE** - A story.

- **NOMA MODEL** - One of Alexander's four models of the relationship between Science and Religion: the idea that Science and Religion are asking different questions which do not overlap.

- **POST-MODERNISM** - School of thought following on from, and reacting to, modernity. The essential "truth" of postmodernism is that "there is no truth." It is relativistic.

SELF-ASSESSMENT QUESTIONS

1. How do you define "Truth"?

2. Outline Alexander's four models of Science and Religion.

3. Which of Alexander's models do you find most useful?

4. Examine the claim that evolution is a "meta-narrative" on a par with religious understandings of "creation".

5. How does the imagination and imaginal help us understand the commonality between Science and Religion?

6. "You can only be a religious scientist to the extent to which you are prepared to ignore the truth claims of either science or religion." Assess this view.

7. Summarise the chapter on Origins in 1,000 words.

8. Summarise the chapter on Design Arguments in 1,000 words.

9. Summarise the chapter on Miracles in 1,000 words.

10. Write your response to an article entitled "Science OR Religion?"

Postscript

Tristan Stone studied Theology at Cambridge University before embarking upon his teaching career. He has taught Philosophy, English and Music in schools and colleges across Kent and will be responsible for Philosophy, Theology and Ethics at the Harris Westminster Sixth Form which opens in September 2014. In addition to writing for PushMe Press, Tristan has written and produced four plays and is working on a series of Young Adult novels.

Lightning Source UK Ltd.
Milton Keynes UK
UKOW04f0712190914

238795UK00001B/15/P